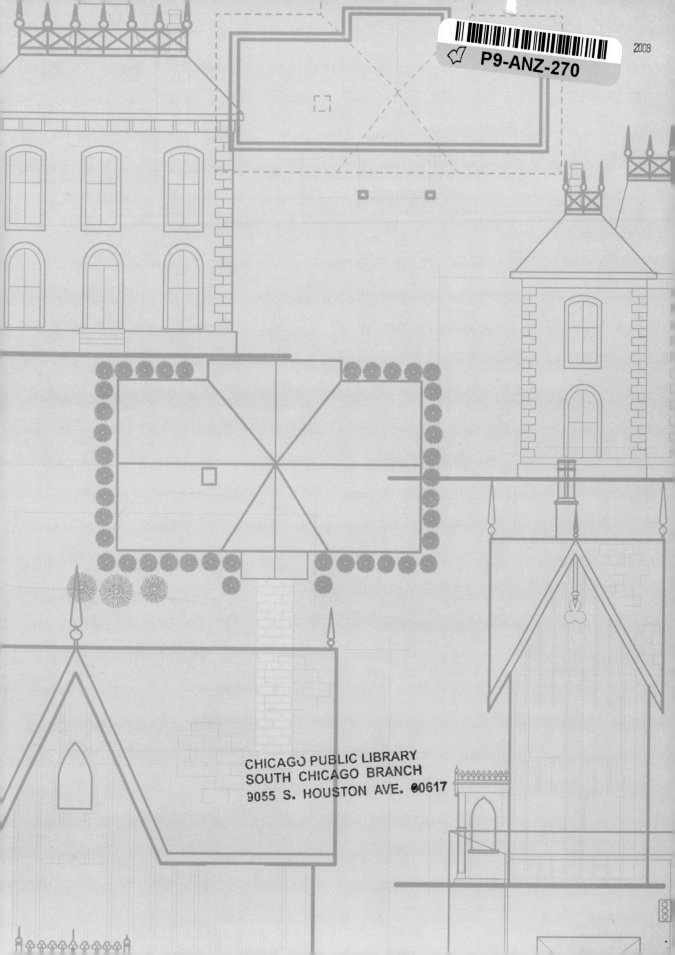

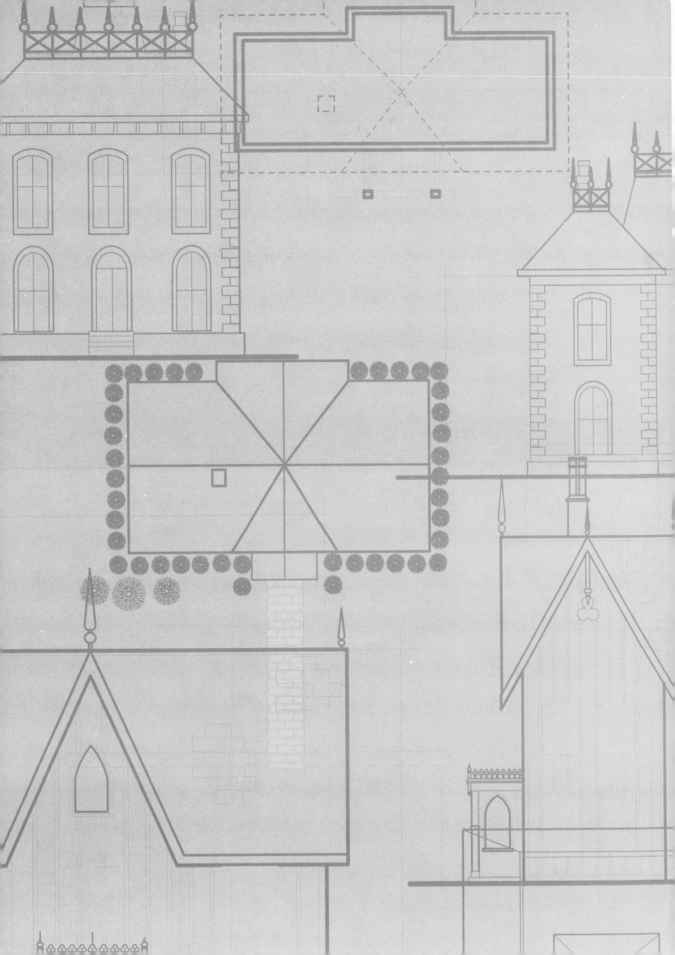

THE

GINGERBREAD
ARCHITECT

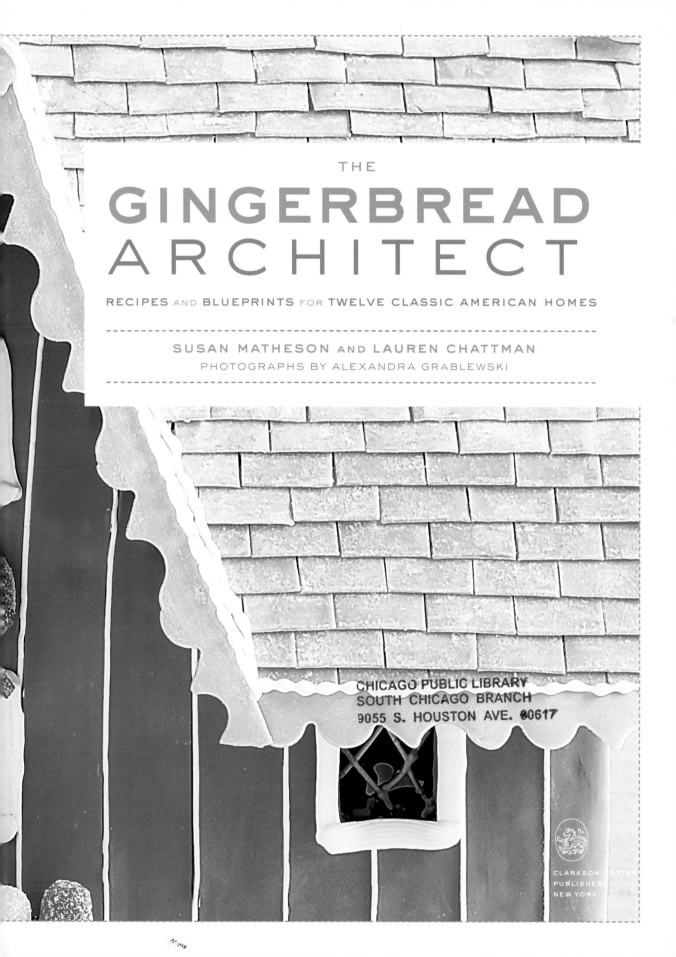

THE
GINGERBREAD
ARCHITECT

RECIPES AND BLUEPRINTS FOR TWELVE CLASSIC AMERICAN HOMES

SUSAN MATHESON AND LAUREN CHATTMAN
PHOTOGRAPHS BY ALEXANDRA GRABLEWSKI

CLARKSON POTTER
PUBLISHERS
NEW YORK

Published in the United States by Clarkson Potter/Publishers, an imprint of the Crown Publishing Group, a division of Random House, Inc., New York.
www.crownpublishing.com
www.clarksonpotter.com

Clarkson N. Potter is a trademark and Potter and colophon are registered trademarks of Random House, Inc.

Library of Congress Cataloging-in-Publication Data
Matheson, Susan
  The gingerbread architect : recipes and blueprints for twelve classic American homes / Susan Matheson and Lauren Chattman. — 1st ed.
  Includes index.
  1. Gingerbread houses.   I. Chattman, Lauren.   II. Title.
TX771.M314875   2008
641.7'1—dc22   2008006769

ISBN 978-0-307-40678-1

Printed in China

Design by Laura Palese

10 9 8 7 6 5 4 3 2 1

First Edition

CONTENTS

INTRODUCTION
6

EQUIPMENT
81
INGREDIENTS
82
THE RECIPES
83
THE TEMPLATES
87

INTRODUCTION

IF YOU HAVE PICKED UP THIS BOOK, CHANCES ARE THE WINTER HOLIDAYS ARE APPROACHING. Maybe you're sitting in a bookstore, taking a breather from the madness all around you at the shopping mall. Wouldn't it be great to be at home in the kitchen, making something festive and beautiful? Isn't that what the season is all about?

The Gingerbread Architect is a complete guide for anyone—from beginners to experienced bakers—who would like to redirect some energy toward creating something special and sweet to celebrate this wonderful time of year. A from-scratch gingerbread house is the ultimate holiday baking project. Sure, it takes work. But the rewards are priceless. Your pride in your accomplishment will be matched only by the delight of everyone who stops by to admire your masterpiece. It goes without saying that you will be a hero to your children and their friends.

These gingerbread houses are a little different from others you may have seen. When an architect who is also an avid baker gets together with a house-obsessed pastry chef, the result is a passionate discussion of how to build a better gingerbread house. That's how this book began—with the two of us fantasizing about gingerbread houses that would be more fun and interesting than the usual slope-roofed buildings covered with dime-store candy featured in supermarket checkout magazines every December. We longed to build houses that were more than "decorated sheds," to use architect Robert Venturi's expression, with candy and icing applied in uninspiring and unevocative ways. As Venturi also said, "Less is a bore." Our wish was for house plans that would satisfy our desire for good design without skimping on that seasonal imperative, excessive sugar.

One of us lives in a turn-of-the-century city brownstone and the other in a modest Victorian farmhouse, so we started there, with two authentic house styles that we loved. Could they be rendered in gingerbread? What were the technical difficulties? How could they be embellished with candy and still remain true to their sources? We liked the idea of starting with a real model, and we talked about which other classic American houses would be fun to make in gingerbread. The list quickly grew to include a Cape Cod, an Adirondack camp cottage, and an antebellum plantation. Wouldn't it be fun to have not just templates for the pieces but actual architectural blueprints to help us envision the finished products?

And then we started to build our houses, modifying the plans as we worked. To casual listeners, our conversations must have sounded a tad obsessive: Would it be historically inaccurate to shingle the roof of a Tudor revival with shredded wheat, even though American examples of this style are rarely thatched? Which would be more realistic: a rock candy or a marzipan cactus sprouting up in the turbinado sugar sand outside a gingerbread pueblo house?

But we never lost sight of the ultimate goal: to have fun and make our families smile. We may have sweated over the creation of the characteristically curved facade on our South Beach Art Deco House, but our real pleasure was in dreaming up whimsical embellishments like the pink flamingo cookies with fruit leather Santa hats standing outside. The fact is that neither of us would have developed an interest in the

subject if we weren't also bringing up children and looking for ways to celebrate the holidays with them in the kitchen. Baking cookies is great, but there's no better seasonal project than making an exquisite gingerbread house. Our girls went crazy for each and every house we dreamed up, and their delighted response was enough to keep us going through all twelve of them.

We have done our best to put together recipes and blueprints to help you build your own dream gingerbread house with as little stress as possible. Along the way, we made a lot of mistakes. The roof of a house shingled with Andes mints collapsed. After we wept, we rebuilt it and reshingled it with lighter Oreo Thin Crisps. The Tootsie Roll palm trees for another house looked fantastic but kept flopping over. Because we wanted the landscape to say "holiday," not "hurricane," we got rid of them and made new ones from cookie dough. Once we worked out the kinks, we were thrilled with every one of our creations. And, in the end, we realized we had drafted plans not only for twelve gingerbread houses but also for an annual ritual. Neither of us can now imagine a holiday season without a gingerbread house. We hope you will have so much fun building your own house this year that you will want to bake and frost your way toward a new dream gingerbread house every winter, creating a holiday tradition of your own.

HISTORICAL ACCURACY AND REINTERPRETATION IN GINGERBREAD

The biggest challenge in drawing the plans was to give each house the recognizable features of an Adirondack, Second Empire, or modernist home, for example, but to simplify the design so that each was doable in gingerbread. Certain design elements, like the Adirondack Camp's stone chimney, were easy to incorporate. Others, like the Greek Revival Antebellum Plantation's many porches and balconies, fell away for the sake of practicality.

These buildings aren't architectural models, after all, but gingerbread houses. We use design shorthand and a sense of humor to telegraph a particular house's provenance. It's hard to take your work too seriously when your construction materials are pretzel rods, licorice allsorts, and fruit leather, your paving stones are Necco wafers or pieces of Bazooka bubble gum, and your landscape elements are spearmint leaves and marshmallows!

Accompanying each recipe is a historical note on the particular style of the house, with a brief and necessarily general discussion of when and where the style originated, the circumstances of its origin, and its basic features. We also provide a description of our reinterpretation of the style in gingerbread, listing the elements we included to mark the house as, say, a brownstone or a Cape.

In a note on construction, we write about any challenges we had in putting together the house. With the benefit of our experience, you can avoid many of the difficulties we encountered and mistakes we made. You won't forget to etch the outlines of your Cape Cod foundation stones before you put the house together, as Lauren did, forcing her to pipe them without a guide. When building the Adirondack Camp chimney, you will know, as Susan did not, to adjust the size of the chimney pieces if you are planning to use particularly large candy rocks to cover it.

Additionally, we supply a list of features that didn't make it into our rendering but that you should feel free to incorporate if you want to vary our design. If you are more ambitious and energetic than we were, you may add carved niches and low benches to your Pueblo House, add stained glass to the windows of your Carpenter Gothic, or substitute edible gold leaf cut in an abstract Egyptian design for the simple starfish border on the South Beach Art Deco House, for example.

We hope you will page through this book as you would page through a home magazine or a book of architectural plans, choosing a design that fits your needs and modifying it to suit your taste. There's no reason the evergreen tree we use in front of the Greek Revival Antebellum

Plantation wouldn't look great outside the Victorian Farmhouse, or the jelly-ring wreath on the Carpenter Gothic couldn't decorate the door of the Second Empire House. The licorice roof on the Cape Cod could just as well shingle the roof of the Adirondack Camp, and so on. And, of course, there are a million clever ways to decorate a gingerbread house that we haven't thought of, but you surely will once you begin.

HOW MANY GINGERBREAD MEN DOES IT TAKE TO BUILD A GINGERBREAD HOUSE?

Style considerations may be of secondary importance to novice gingerbread house builders or bakers in a hurry. If that's you, you might want to choose a house on the simple side, such as the Cape Cod or the Dawson City House. Conversely, you might be up for the challenge of putting together a real puzzle of a house like the Modern, or making pastillage to decorate the Urban Brownstone. We've rated each house with a degree of difficulty from one gingerbread man to four—from simple to more elaborate—to guide you in your choice as you look through this book.

THE CONSTRUCTION SCHEDULE

Monticello wasn't built in a day, so don't expect to build your plantation in twenty-four hours. It's best to spread out the project over a week to minimize stress and maximize fun. We recommend the following plan if you want to build your house at a relaxed pace. (If you prefer to compress the schedule, you can shop and mix the dough on Day 1, cut the templates and bake the pieces on Day 2, assemble the house on Day 3, and decorate on Day 4. But if you are going to do this, you might have to send your family away and tell them not to return until you are finished, which sort of defeats the purpose of building a gingerbread house in the first place!)

DAY 1: SHOP Devote a day to gathering materials. If your supermarket is well stocked, you may be able to buy everything you need for a simpler house there, including baking supplies, equipment, and candy. But you may have to make a trip to a kitchenware store for large baking sheets, a rolling pin, and other equipment, and to a well-stocked candy store (we like the ones that sell bulk candy from bins, especially when the bins are organized by color) for just the right decorations. If the house you choose requires items that might not be available locally, such as sheet gelatin, fondant, or a fondant cutter, order them at least a week before you want to begin construction.

DAY 2: MIX THE DOUGH You may need several batches, which you can make consecutively in the mixer, without washing it in between. Once mixed, the dough must be chilled for at least three hours and up to three days. We like to make the dough at least one day in advance of baking.

DAY 3: CUT THE TEMPLATES You can enlarge the templates on a copy machine by 400 percent or use graph paper and the measurements given to draw them at home. Then, trace them onto thin cardboard so they are sturdy enough to work with. In either case, give yourself a few hours and take care to double-check them for accuracy (the length of the walls is important; the precise placement of windows not so much) before cutting the templates with sharp scissors or a straight-edged razor.

DAY 4: BAKE THE GINGERBREAD Rolling out the dough, using the templates to cut all of the pieces, baking them, cooling them, and wrapping them in plastic will take the better part of a morning or an afternoon.

DAY 5: ASSEMBLE THE HOUSE Each step takes only minutes, but it is often necessary to let the icing dry after gluing certain pieces together before going farther. So plan for a lot of downtime in between steps.

DAYS 6 AND 7: DECORATE Finally, the fun part! This can take a few hours or up to two days, depending on how elaborate your decorations are.

Whichever house you choose, carefully read the recipe through several times before you begin, as you may have to modify this basic schedule depending on a particular construction. Sometimes decorating must be done preconstruction. For example, the roof of the Dawson City House needs to be iced and dipped in a pan of sanding sugar before it is set atop the walls. You don't want to put the roof on and then start throwing handfuls of sugar at it.

USING THE BLUEPRINTS AND TEMPLATES

The blueprints are here to help you envision your house and then put it together. The finely drawn details in the elevations show what the house looks like in our minds. While it is impossible to show all sides of a house in the photographs, the elevation drawings depict every side, giving you a complete picture of each house. The drawings in combination with the photos will make excellent guides for your gingerbread crafting.

The templates show the exact dimensions of each gingerbread piece you will need to construct your house. Your local copy shop will be an essential stop in creating your own set of cardboard templates. There you can enlarge the templates 400 percent. Check the final enlarged template images against the measurements given in the book. (Alternatively, you can choose to make your house smaller or even larger than we have directed, but please make certain that all your template pieces are enlarged by the same percentage so they fit together in the end.) Once you have used the paper templates to make cardboard templates, we highly recommend taping the cardboard pieces together before you start cutting out your dough, just to make sure you've cut them accurately and you understand how the pieces will fit together once they are baked. You may want to enlarge the floor plans that are included in the template sec-

tion to place under the test cardboard template house as an extra check. Don't discard your cardboard templates once you are finished cutting the gingerbread. If one of your chimney pieces goes mysteriously missing (dogs, small children, and grandfathers are all suspects, in our experience) before you have attached it to your house, you will have the template ready to cut a new piece in no time.

WORKING WITH GINGERBREAD DOUGH

The dough recipe we use (page 83) is made with vegetable shortening for durability, molasses for rich flavor and color, and abundant ground ginger, cinnamon, and cloves for spice. It has enough baking powder to lighten it a little, but not so much that it will spread significantly and become larger than the templates.

Don't be afraid to mix the dough until all the ingredients are well combined and smooth. Undermixing may result in a crumbly dough. If this happens, you can return the dough to the mixer or knead it by hand on the counter until it is silky and workable.

Once mixed, the dough should be allowed to firm up in the refrigerator for a few hours. It will keep, well wrapped in plastic, for up to three days. You can even make the dough up to one month in advance, wrap it, freeze it, and defrost it overnight in the refrigerator before rolling and baking. Each recipe calls for more than enough dough for each house. Wrap the scraps and refrigerate or freeze them. You never know when you will have a dough emergency, and if you have extra on hand, you will be prepared. Once your house is completed, you can always use leftover dough to make gingerbread men to decorate your Christmas tree (see page 85).

As easy as the dough is to work with, you should still roll it directly onto parchment paper, cut it into pieces, and then slide the paper, with the pieces, right onto rimless baking sheets. This way there's no risk of tearing or stretching the dough as you might if you tried to transfer large pieces

from a work surface to a baking sheet without the support of parchment paper. Additionally, the crushed hard candies we like to use as window glass will stick to any non-parchment surface, including greased baking sheets and heavy-duty aluminum foil. If you plan on melting candies inside your window openings, it is absolutely necessary to use parchment paper. Sprinkle the parchment with flour, and then sprinkle the top of the dough with more flour before rolling. If your rolling pin starts to stick to the dough, sprinkle with more flour. When you are finished rolling and cutting, use a soft-bristled pastry brush to gently brush away any excess flour before baking. Don't forget to score the unbaked dough if you'd like to bake in a brick, stone, or other pattern.

Bake the gingerbread pieces until they are nice and firm. You don't want them to be too soft. Small pieces, like doors and chimneys, will take about ten minutes. Larger pieces will take a few minutes longer. Slide the pieces, still on the parchment, onto wire racks to cool completely; then transfer them to baking sheets and wrap the sheets in plastic. You can store the pieces this way for up to one week, or even longer if your kitchen is cool and dry.

Our dough recipe is designed so that the pieces will puff a little bit but won't spread significantly. If your dough is rolled out unevenly, however, the thinner sections may be pulled by the thicker sections, resulting in uneven edges. If the edges of your pieces don't look as straight coming out of the oven as they did going in, slide the warm dough onto a cutting board, place the template over the piece, and trim the edges with a sharp knife before the dough cools and while it is still soft. Then transfer to a rack to cool completely.

As you begin to assemble your house, you may find that even if you trimmed your dough when it came out of the oven, the edges are not as straight as you would like them to be and don't come

together to make neat enough corners. If this is the case, you can use a handheld grater to very gently smooth the edges once the gingerbread has completely cooled. Go slowly and check your pieces against each other often, so you don't break them or grate away too much.

ASSEMBLY

You'll need a sturdy platform for your house. There are several choices. When we could, we used heavy-duty wooden or plastic cutting boards we already owned. For the larger houses, like the Carpenter Gothic and the Pueblo House, a board measuring 16 x 20 inches gave us enough room for the house and a little landscaping. For smaller buildings, like the Adirondack Camp or the Cape Cod, a cutting board measuring 12 x 16 was sufficient. When we ran out of cutting boards (which happened when we had several houses under construction at once) we had heavy-duty Styrofoam cut to our specifications at a craft store and covered the board with aluminum foil. (Just in case our children wanted to eat pieces of the house at a later date, we didn't want them ingesting bits of the foam they might pull off along with the candy and cookies.) Another alternative is a cake drum designed for heavy cakes and gingerbread houses and already covered with embossed foil (see Resources, page 86). In every recipe, we give measurements for the board you will need for a particular house.

Work slowly and deliberately when assembling your house. Before you begin, figure out where you want your house to sit on the board. Take a quick measure to make sure all the pieces will fit. Embarrassing as it is to admit, Lauren at first positioned the facade of her Pueblo House at a nice distance from the front of the board to accommodate the

cactus garden and terrazzo walkway she had in mind, only realizing when she got around to attaching the rear facade that she was an inch short on available real estate!

The walls and roof of every house can be glued together with plain white icing. In some cases, such as with the Pueblo House, which is covered with clay-colored stucco, or the Tudor Revival, which is covered in white stucco, more icing applied later will cover up most of the spots where two pieces of gingerbread are joined. In other cases, such as with the Adirondack Camp or the Victorian Farmhouse, the gingerbread is hardly covered. For the most seamless look on these houses, you might consider tinting a portion of your icing with food coloring to match the brown of your gingerbread.

Before you start piping icing onto your pieces, pile some heavy mugs or cans right beside you to support the pieces as you stand them on the board. Make sure your box of straight pins is handy and open also, so you can grab one when you need to pin two pieces together as the icing gluing them to each other dries. Especially during the early stages, it's helpful to have an extra set of hands, even little ones, to hold pieces in place.

Heed instructions to let icing dry before proceeding to the next phase of construction. It is dangerous to attach the roof before the walls are strongly bonded together: The weight of the roof might cause the walls to shift. In the worst-case scenario the entire structure, if not securely pinned, may tumble down.

Don't panic if you find an occasional gap between pieces. As long as most of a piece's edge connects with another piece's edge, the house will hold, and gaps can be filled in with extra icing. Do your best to work neatly, but remember that most little mistakes can be covered by icing and

Using cans and mugs to stand walls upright

Pinning pieces together while the icing dries

decorations—and even if the gaps are visible in the end, a gingerbread house is most pleasing when it looks handmade.

DECORATION

We love the austere beauty of the gingerbread blueprints, but, as you can see from the photos in this book, we also love adding color to the finished houses with icing and lots of candy. The blueprints look just like real house plans, with finely drawn details like window trim, roof shingles, and shutters. The challenge is in translating the drawings into a gingerbread house, using icing and candy to render the details. There are no hard-and-fast rules when it comes to decorating, but here are a few approaches we have used successfully:

CHOOSE A DOMINANT COLOR

When researching art deco style, we saw that various shades of green were often used on the kind of house we wanted to re-create in gingerbread. Once we settled on a pale green stucco for the exterior, the rest of the candy and icing details just fell into place. Other pastels—the pale yellow and lavender for the star border, the pale pink for the window grates—matched the pale green. A darker jade green for the door and door trim added authenticity to the color palette. The bright green fruit leather palm fronds harmonized with the more muted greens. The one discordant color note—the flamingos' Santa hats—is a playful comment on the very un-Arctic weather in Miami.

PLAY WITH CONTRASTS Contrasting two colors can result in an eye-catching effect. Violet and yellow are certainly not historically accurate, but they really pop when used together on the Dawson City House.

TAKE INSPIRATION FROM A FAVORITE CANDY We knew we wanted to use black licorice Twizzlers for the half-timbers on our Tudor Revival house, and the rest of the decorating became simple when we spotted a bag of licorice allsorts. The colorful candies, all with a touch of black, became paving stones, pinnacles, and trim boards for a variegated but put-together look.

PUNCH UP NEUTRAL COLORS It is possible to decorate a house like the Adirondack Camp, which is traditionally constructed from natural materials, with a similar palette of candies—chocolate or candy rocks, pretzels, and Tootsie Rolls molded into decorative trim. The effect is striking and elegant. To please children and prevent this type of house from becoming too drab, be sure to add a few colorful touches, like a bright blue door and a red mailbox flag.

WHEN IN DOUBT, THINK CHRISTMAS It is nice, occasionally, to use traditional green and red. We don't like to go overboard, instead adding small touches like the Kelly green shutters and red shingles on the Cape Cod. When we do choose to work with Christmas colors exclusively, as in the Greek Revival Antebellum Plantation, which has red-and-white peppermint-stick columns, green shingles, and red sugared fruit strip pediment decoration, we want the candies and colors to harmonize rather than compete.

DON'T FORGET TO LANDSCAPE Even the smallest landscaping detail finishes a house beautifully. Add a little pretzel fence, a marshmallow shrubbery hedge, a single evergreen tree made by covering an upside-down ice cream sugar cone with piped icing leaves, or even just a mailbox and a short walkway to the front door and your house will take on a finished look that it was lacking even

when fully decorated. We've provided simple suggestions for each of our houses that can be adapted endlessly to suit your own uniquely decorated house.

THINK ABOUT THE REAR FACADE These houses were designed to be viewed from all sides, and the back of each house is decorated accordingly. Stucco, siding, back doors and windows, and other trimmings are included in the plans and recipes. If you plan to display your house against a wall and would like to save a significant amount of time, you may cut back on or eliminate these decorations.

A NOTE ABOUT WINDOWS

We wanted our houses to be completely edible, so at the beginning of this project we ruled out using materials such as cellophane to stand in for window glass. Sometimes we keep it simple and use nothing at all. The Pueblo House doesn't cry out for window glass; fruit leather lintels are all that is needed to finish the windows. For the Cape Cod and the Greek Revival Antebellum Plantation, thin strips of chewing gum become mullions, filling the window spaces so no glass is necessary. Two houses, the Carpenter Gothic and the Tudor Revival, look great with small diamond-shaped window panes. Here we use sheet gelatin (see page 82), which is clear but with a diamond pattern imprinted on it, to stand in for glass. Gelatin is also a clever stand-in for the curved window glass in the South Beach Art Deco House, as it is flexible enough to keep that shape.

We wanted to try illuminating a couple of houses from within with battery-powered lights (see opposite for details). In these cases, windows made of melted butterscotch or caramel hard candy glow beautifully. After experimenting with ways of melting the candy, we settled on this one: First, bake your gingerbread pieces until firm. Then, remove the baking sheet from the oven and sprinkle the crushed candy into the window spaces in a thin layer so it completely covers the parchment. Brush any candy on the edges of the gingerbread into the window space. Return the baking sheet to the oven until the candy melts, about five minutes. If after five minutes you see holes in the windows, cover the holes with a little more crushed candy and return to the oven for a minute. Let the gingerbread cool completely on the baking sheets, to give the candy glass time to harden before proceeding with the recipe.

LIGHTING YOUR GINGERBREAD HOUSE

Melted candy windows look especially nice at night when you've taken the time to light your house from within. Buy a small floral lighting set, which includes a string of eight to twelve tiny lightbulbs on a cord with a battery pack at one end (see the photograph on page 61). The bulbs don't throw off enough heat to soften the gingerbread or the candy. The battery pack remains outside the house, so you can remove the batteries to turn the lights on and off and replace batteries if necessary. (Some of the packs have an on/off switch.) Here are instructions for building your house around a set of these lights:

1. Cut 2 pieces of heavy (corrugated) cardboard so that they are the same size as the board you will be using for your house. Cut a hole through the two layers, in the center, making an opening just large enough to pull the lights through.

2. Glue the two layers of cardboard together, aligning the center holes and the outer edges. Cut a ½-inch-wide strip out of the bottom layer, extending from the hole to what will be the back side of the board. Pull the lights through the hole and run the cord inside the cutout strip so that the wire is concealed on the underside and the battery pack is off the board. Tape the cord in place. Cover the two layers in aluminum foil, allowing the lights and the wires of the battery pack to pass through a corresponding hole in the foil.

3. As you build your house around the lights, you can direct them so that they illuminate all of the windows. Wrap the bulbs on their cord around a pretzel rod, pointing them in various directions depending on the house you are building, and secure the pretzel rod to the cardboard with Royal Icing or duct tape before attaching the final wall or the roof. Or string the lights around the interior, securing them to the walls with straight pins.

HISTORIC PRESERVATION

Every square inch of each gingerbread house is completely edible, so it is up to you to decide if and when you want to start nibbling at it. In the meantime, display it in a cool, dry place, out of direct sunlight, to keep the decorations from falling off and the gingerbread from softening. Don't be alarmed if a jelly bean or a licorice twist comes loose. It is easy enough to make minor repairs with a bit of Royal Icing.

Where we live, in the chilly Northeast, the forced-air heating in our homes dries out our gingerbread so it becomes rock hard and almost impossible to break. (In Sweden, where the climate is even colder, there is actually a postholiday custom of taking a sledgehammer to the gingerbread house to say good-bye to Christmas spirits.) The softening of the gingerbread is a problem only in warm, humid climates, where the cookie can sponge up the moisture in the air. If it is humid where you live, or if you plan to store your house and bring it out again next year, you may consider prolonging its life by spraying it with an acrylic sealer (available at craft stores) to keep moisture out. Choose a sealer with a matte finish rather than a shiny one for the most natural look. Carefully carry the house to a well-ventilated area in the garage or the basement and set it on newspaper before spraying it and allowing it to dry. Remember, of course, that treating your house this way will render it inedible!

For long-term storage, carefully lower your house into a cardboard box and loosely cover it, allowing air to circulate around it, before tucking it away in a closet or other safe, out-of-the-way location. Storing it in the basement or the attic is not recommended—the extreme temperatures will compromise its structure before the year is up.

 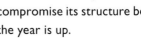

PUEBLO HOUSE

SEE TEMPLATES ON PAGE 87

With its EARTH-COLORED PLASTER FINISH, this style lends itself beautifully to a rendering in gingerbread. Its distinctive features—A FLAT ROOF made of cedar logs (pretzel logs protruding from the facade represent these), ladders (made of pretzel sticks), and HOLES IN THE ROOF providing access to the upper level—are not difficult to construct. The house is covered with adobe-colored icing (brown with undertones of yellow and pink). "Bricks" etched into the unbaked gingerbread are left exposed in places to suggest the antiquity of the structure. A Taos blue door, a large cactus made of green rock candy, succulent plants in terra-cotta pots, and a terrazzo walkway made out of striped Sour Power Belts cut and laid as tile are authentic and whimsical touches.

INGREDIENTS

- 1½ RECIPES GINGER-BREAD DOUGH (PAGE 83), CHILLED
- 2½ RECIPES ROYAL ICING (PAGE 84)

  BLUE, GREEN, BROWN, AND PINK FOOD COLORING
- 20 RED HOTS CANDIES (FROM 1 2½-OUNCE BOX)

  ABOUT 25 MINI PRETZEL STICKS, EACH ABOUT 4 INCHES LONG (FROM 1 12-OUNCE BAG)
- 2 (12.75 OUNCE) BAGS PRETZEL RODS
- 3 1 x ¼-INCH PIECES DARK CHERRY FRUIT LEATHER (FROM 1 1½-OUNCE PACKAGE)
- 5 PINK-AND-GREEN-STRIPED SOUR POWER BELTS (1½ OUNCES)
- ¼ CUP TURBINADO SUGAR, SUCH AS SUGAR IN THE RAW
- 4 BLACK LICORICE NIBS
- 1 BLUE TWIZZLER
- 1 YELLOW TWIZZLER

  SEVERAL LARGE PIECES GREEN ROCK CANDY
- 9 BURNT PEANUTS
- 6 PINK JELLY RINGS
- 4 WATERMELON-FLAVORED LICORICE STIX
- 1 WATERMELON GUM BALL
- 1 HARIBO RASPBERRY CANDY
- 2 RED LICORICE SHOELACES
- 25 MINI M&MS (FROM 1 1.8-OUNCE TUBE)
- 7 GREEN APPLE GUM BALLS

CONSTRUCTION NOTE

To support the inset roof, which is set an inch or so below the walls, you will need to glue pretzel rods into each interior corner of the house. Give them adequate time to dry (at least 4 hours) and then drop the roof into place. The pretzels and icing together will be strong enough to hold up the roof.

special equipment

16 x 20-INCH CUTTING BOARD OR FOIL-COVERED STYROFOAM BOARD

PASTRY BAG AND #7 PLAIN TIP

HISTORICAL NOTE

The pueblo house is a descendant of ancient multifamily houses built of sun-dried brick by the Pueblo Indians in what is now the American Southwest. When Spanish conquistadores arrived they adapted the style, adding porches held up with wooden posts, heavy wooden doors, and carved wooden corbels (short horizontal timbers supporting a girder) to give their houses an old-world touch. Pueblo Revival (commonly known as Santa Fe) style became popular in and around New Mexico in the early 1900s and is still going strong today. The new pueblo buildings, made of stucco-covered building block rather than genuine adobe, celebrate the architectural heritage of the area and continue to promote the state's identity and advertise its allure.

more pueblo style

Our house incorporates several elements of pueblo style, including a flat, inset roof with no overhang, stepped levels, spouts to direct rainwater, simple windows, *vigas* (heavy timbers), and ladders. To embellish your house, you could add other pueblo and Santa Fe style elements, including:

- A rounded parapet (a low protective wall at the edge of a balcony or the roof).

- Low benches protruding from the walls (cut from gingerbread and supported with gingerbread braces).

- Niches carved out of the walls to display religious objects (use your imagination to create these from candies).

1. **BAKE THE GINGERBREAD:** Enlarge the templates on pieces of thin cardboard or sturdy paper and cut to size. Preheat the oven to 375°F.

2. Divide the dough into 5 equal pieces. Wrap 4 pieces tightly in plastic wrap and keep in the refrigerator. Lightly flour a piece of parchment paper and roll out the fifth piece of dough onto the parchment so it is $\frac{1}{4}$ inch thick. Place the template for the smaller front piece of the house (piece E) on the dough and cut around the template with a sharp knife. Cut away the door opening and set aside the door piece. Use the dull edge of a knife to score a small section of the front to look like bricks. Remove the scraps from the parchment, wrap them in plastic, and refrigerate.

3. Slide the parchment onto a rimless baking sheet. Place the door piece next to the front piece on the baking sheet, at least 1 inch away from it. Slide the baking sheet into the oven and bake until the door is firm, about 10 minutes. Use a metal spatula to remove the door to a wire rack to cool. Continue to bake piece E until the edges are lightly browned and the center is firm, 2 to 4 minutes more. Slide the parchment onto a wire rack and let the gingerbread cool completely.

4. Working in 4 batches and using the remaining 4 pieces of dough plus scraps, repeat the rolling and baking with the larger front (piece D), rear piece (A), 4 sides (B, C, F, and G), and roof pieces, scoring a small section of the back and the largest side piece as described above.

5. When the pieces are cool, transfer them to baking sheets and tightly cover the sheets in plastic until you are ready to assemble the house. They will keep for up to 1 week.

6. **COLOR AND DECORATE THE DOOR:** Place $\frac{1}{4}$ cup icing in a small bowl and tint with blue food coloring and a little bit of green food coloring to achieve a Taos blue (a turquoise). Use a small offset spatula to ice the door piece with the blue icing. Arrange 13 Red Hots about $\frac{1}{2}$ inch from the sides and top of the door to resemble door studs. Set aside to dry for at least 2 hours.

7. **MAKE THE LADDERS:** Fit the pastry bag with the #7 plain tip and fill with icing. Keep the rest of the icing in a bowl, pressing a piece of plastic wrap against the surface to prevent it from drying out. Line a baking sheet with parchment paper. For the large ladder, use icing to glue 3 mini pretzel sticks end to end on top of the parchment. Glue another 3 mini pretzel sticks end to end, setting them parallel to the first 3, about 3 inches apart. Glue 13 mini pretzel sticks at even intervals to the 2 rows to connect them. For the small ladder, arrange 2 mini pretzel sticks parallel to each other and about 3 inches apart. Glue 4 mini pretzel sticks at even intervals to the parallel mini pretzel sticks to connect them. Set aside to dry for at least 2 hours.

8. **ASSEMBLE THE HOUSE:** If you are illuminating your house, see page 13. Pipe icing along the bottom edge of the back piece of the house (piece A). Position it where you want it to stand on your board and place a heavy mug or can on each side to help it stand upright until the icing dries. Pipe icing along the bottom edge and back edge of the largest side piece (piece B) and attach the side to the front so that the side edge of the side is flush against the back of the front piece. Repeat with the side C piece. Attach piece D to the front corner of piece C and middle of side piece B,

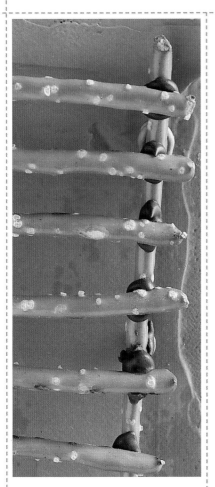

adding more mugs for support as necessary. Insert straight pins through the back wall into each side wall. Let stand for at least ½ hour to dry. Wrap the tip of the pastry bag with plastic wrap and refrigerate until ready to continue. Remove the mugs and pins.

9. **ATTACH THE FRONT AND SIDE WALLS:** Pipe icing along the bottom edge and longer side edge of the smaller front facade E piece. Attach to the side B piece so that the side edge of the front piece is flush against the side edge of the side piece. Pipe icing along the side edges and bottom edge of the side wall piece F and attach so that one side edge meets the corner of piece E and the other attaches to the front side of piece D.

10. **CONSTRUCT THE ROOF SUPPORTS AND ATTACH THE ROOF:** Cut off ¾ inch from the end of each pretzel rod and reserve. Pipe icing along one side of a large pretzel rod and glue it into an interior corner of the house. Add an extra piece of another pretzel rod so the 2 pretzel rods together extend to 1 inch below the roof. Repeat with the remaining pretzel rods so there is a rod in every interior corner that extends to 1 inch below the roof. Repeat for the front section, installing an additional set of pretzel supports, one along the interior middle of the front facade (piece F) and one directly opposite it along the exterior of front wall piece D. Let dry for at least 4 hours.

11. **ATTACH ROOF PIECES 1 AND 2:** Pipe icing onto the underside corners of roof pieces 1 and 2 and drop them into place so each corner is resting on a pretzel-rod support. Let dry for 1 hour.

12. **ATTACH THE ELEVATED STONE WALL:** Pipe icing along the sides and bottom of side wall G and attach to roof piece 2 and front wall pieces E and D. Install pretzel roof supports to come 1 inch below the top of piece G. Let dry for 1 hour.

13. **ATTACH ROOF 3:** Pipe icing on to the underside corners of roof piece 3 and drop into place. Let dry for 1 hour.

14. **STUCCO THE HOUSE:** Place 3½ cups icing in a medium bowl and use a few drops of brown food coloring with a touch of pink to achieve an adobe red. Use a small offset spatula to spread a thin layer over the entire house, leaving the brick patches exposed. Stick the pretzel rod ends, rounded ends exposed, along the top edges of each facade piece. Place a fruit leather lintel over each window (except for the one with a wreath). Let stand to dry for 1 hour.

15. **ATTACH THE DOORS:** Pipe icing on the back edge of the doors and at the edges and glue to the doorways.

16. **LAY THE TILE WALKWAY:** Place 1 cup or more icing (depending on how large your board is)

in a medium bowl and use a little brown food coloring to tint it a light brown. Spread the light brown icing over the exposed board. Cut the Sour Power Belts into ¾-inch tiles, trimming as necessary, and lay them down in a parquet pattern to create the walkway. Sprinkle the turbinado sugar on the icing "sand."

17. MAKE AND ATTACH THE LANTERN FIXTURES: Use a sharp paring knife to trim 2 of the black licorice nibs into lantern shapes. Carve 2 handles out of the remaining 2 licorice nibs. Attach the handles to the lanterns with icing. Cut 2 tiny candles from the blue Twizzler and attach one to each of the lanterns. Cut 2 tiny flames from the yellow Twizzler and attach one to each of the lanterns above each candle. Attach the lanterns to either side of the door with icing.

18. LANDSCAPE THE HOUSE: Use icing to glue a piece of green rock candy to the sand in front of the house. Glue more rock candy on top of the first piece to create a large cactus, resting one arm of the cactus against the side of the house for stability. Decorate the cactus with flowers made of burnt peanuts.

19. To make pots, stack 3 jelly rings on each side of the door, gluing them together and to the sand with icing. Use a sharp paring knife to make 1-inch cuts in the tops of the watermelon Licorice Stix to create flowering succulent plants. Insert the bottoms of the sticks into the pots. With icing, glue the watermelon gum ball to the sand and glue the raspberry candy to the gum ball to create a small flowering cactus.

20. STRING THE LIGHTS: Weave the red licorice laces over and under the pretzel-rod beams, trimming so they hang down a few inches on each side of each end beam. Attach mini M&Ms at even intervals along the licorice laces to create lights.

21. ATTACH THE LADDERS: Carefully prop the tall ladder against the side wall of the house and the short ladder against the front top wall. If your ladders come apart in places, don't worry. Glue them back together as you prop them up, gluing them at intervals to the house.

22. MAKE THE WREATH: Use icing to glue the green apple gum balls in a circle around the top front window to form a wreath. Glue the remaining 7 Red Hots between the gum balls.

CAPE COD

SEE TEMPLATES ON PAGE 91

Our gingerbread version has the Cape's most recognizable features: a SIMPLE RECTANGULAR FORM, a STONE FOUNDATION made with three colors of piped icing, a CENTER ENTRY DOOR, a large central CHIMNEY clad in brick-red fruit leather, a steep SHINGLED ROOF that doesn't protrude much from the exterior walls of the house, and MULLIONED windows (windows divided into a grid). Cape Cods don't have a lot of exterior ornamentation. SHUTTERS made of icing-covered saltine halves add some color, as do window-box flowers made by piping tiny icing roses onto fresh thyme sprigs inserted into mini Charleston Chews. A MILLSTONE made of chocolate serves as a doorstep.

INGREDIENTS

1 RECIPE GINGER-BREAD DOUGH (PAGE 83), CHILLED

8 STICKS (FROM 1 2¼-OUNCE PACKAGE) JUICY FRUIT GUM

1 RECIPE ROYAL ICING (PAGE 84)

BROWN, RED, GREEN, BLACK, AND PINK FOOD COLORING

2 BLACK LICORICE NIBS

6 SALTINE CRACKERS, CUT IN HALF

3 ½-OUNCE PACKAGES DARK CHERRY FRUIT LEATHER

1 12.4-OUNCE PACKAGE CHOCOLATE-FLAVORED TWIZZLERS, CUT INTO ¾-INCH LENGTHS

6 RED TWIZZLERS, CUT INTO ¾-INCH LENGTHS

1 1½-INCH SQUARE GHIRARDELLI DARK CHOCOLATE OR OTHER DARK CHOCOLATE

6 MINI CHARLESTON CHEWS

1 SMALL BUNCH THYME SPRIGS

34 SMALL YOGURT-COVERED PRETZELS (FROM 1 5-OUNCE BAG)

CONSTRUCTION NOTES

Although you may pipe the foundation stones freehand, it is easier to draw the outlines of the stones with the tip of a sharp paring knife before putting the house together so you have a guide when you are ready to decorate.

If your taste tends toward the minimal, you may skip shingling the roof with Twizzler pieces. Instead, use the dull edge of a knife to score the unbaked roof pieces with horizontal lines every ½ inch.

special equipment

12 x 18-INCH CUTTING BOARD OR FOIL-COVERED STYROFOAM BOARD

PASTRY BAGS AND #7 PLAIN TIP, #4 PLAIN TIP, AND #13 STAR TIP

HISTORICAL
NOTE

This classic American house was first built by English colonists in the 1700s. Based on modest half-timbered English houses, it was built in the New World using local materials. The addition of shutters to the design served to protect the house against New England storms. In the early twentieth century, a revival of the Cape was inspired by a renewed popular interest in colonial history. Economical to build, Colonial Revival Cape Cods were a staple in early suburban housing developments from the 1930s through the 1960s.

1. BAKE THE GINGERBREAD: Enlarge the templates on pieces of thin cardboard or sturdy paper and cut to size. Preheat the oven to 375°F.

2. Divide the dough into 4 equal pieces. Wrap 3 pieces tightly in plastic wrap and keep in the refrigerator. Lightly flour a piece of parchment paper and roll out the fourth piece of dough onto the parchment so it is $\frac{1}{4}$ inch thick. Place the template for the front of the house on the dough and cut around the template with a sharp knife. Cut away the door opening and set aside the door piece. Cut away the windows. Remove the scraps from the parchment, wrap them in plastic, and refrigerate.

3. Slide the parchment onto a rimless baking sheet. Place the door piece next to the front piece on the baking sheet, at least 1 inch away from it. Slide the baking sheet into the oven and bake until the door is firm, about 10 minutes. Use a metal spatula to remove the door to a wire rack to cool. Continue to bake the house until the edges are lightly browned and the center is firm, 2 to 4 minutes more. Slide the parchment onto a wire rack and let cool completely.

4. Working in 3 batches and using the remaining 3 pieces of dough plus scraps, repeat the rolling and baking with the rear, 2 sides, and roof and chimney pieces.

5. When the pieces are cool, transfer them to baking sheets and tightly cover the sheets in plastic until you are ready to assemble the house. They will keep for up to 1 week.

6. ETCH THE FOUNDATION STONES: Use the tip of a sharp paring knife to lightly etch the outlines of the stones that cover the bottom $\frac{3}{4}$ inch of the sides, front, and back of the house.

7. MAKE THE MULLIONED WINDOWS: Use a sharp chef's knife to cut the pieces of gum lengthwise into $\frac{1}{16}$-inch strips. Set aside 12 long strips and cut 9 long strips in half to make 18 short ones. Use icing to glue the strips to the inside of the side, front, and back pieces so they crisscross the windows, 2 long ones going lengthwise and then 3 short ones going crosswise. Set aside for 15 minutes to dry.

8. ASSEMBLE THE HOUSE: If you are illuminating your house, see page 13. Tint about 1 cup icing brown with a few drops of brown food coloring if you like, or use plain white icing. Fit a pastry bag with the #7 plain tip and fill with the icing. Keep the rest of the icing in a bowl, pressing a piece of plastic wrap against the surface to prevent it from drying out. Pipe icing along the bottom edge of the front of the house. Position it where you want it to stand on the board and place a heavy mug or can on each side to help it stand upright until the icing dries. Pipe icing along the bottom edge and front edge of one of the side pieces and attach the side to the front so that the side edge of the side is flush against the back of the front piece. Repeat with the other side and the rear, adding more mugs for support as necessary. Insert straight pins through the front wall into each side wall and through the back wall into each side wall. Wrap the tip of the pastry bag with plastic wrap and refrigerate until you are ready to continue. Let stand until the icing is dry, about 1 hour. Remove the mugs and pins.

9. ATTACH THE ROOF:
Pipe icing along the top edges of the sides and along each side edge of 1 roof piece. Position the roof piece on top of the house, lining it up so its top edge runs from point to point of the sides of the house. Secure the roof piece by inserting straight pins through the front and back of the house and into the roof at the peak and at the eaves. Repeat with the second roof piece. Let stand until the icing is dry, about 1 hour. Remove the pins.

10. ATTACH THE CHIMNEY: Pipe icing on the long sides of the chimney pieces and glue them together to make a rectangular box, standing them vertically upside down until dry. Pipe icing along the bottom edges of

the chimney and attach it at the center of the roof.

11. COLOR THE DOOR AND ATTACH THE HARDWARE: Fill a small bowl with 3 tablespoons icing and tint it brick red, using a few drops of red food coloring along with 1 or 2 drops of brown. Smooth the colored icing over the door. Cut a ⅛-inch-thick slice from one of the licorice nibs and press it into the icing as a doorknob. Cut two ⅛-inch-thick triangles from the other licorice nib for the hinges, and press them into the icing across from the doorknob. Set aside to allow the icing to harden completely, about 2 hours.

12. COLOR THE SHUTTERS: Tint ¼ cup icing green and spread over each of the saltines. Set aside to allow the icing to harden completely, about 1 hour.

13. PIPE THE FOUNDATION STONES: Put 3 tablespoons icing in each of 3 small bowls. Tint the icing in one bowl with 1 or 2 drops of light brown food coloring, another with 5 or 6 drops of dark brown food coloring, and another with 1 or 2 drops of black food coloring to make gray. Cover the surface of two bowls with plastic wrap and transfer the third portion of icing to a pastry bag fitted with the #4 plain

Choose one or more of the following features to add individuality to your Cape Cod gingerbread house:

- While rarely seen on original structures, dormers (small gables projecting from the sloping roof) were often added to later Capes for extra space and light; they are easily added to the roof of the gingerbread house.

- A decorative door, which was often the only ornamental element of the Cape Cod house. Our door is a simple affair, but you can embellish yours with molded pilasters (shallow rectangular columns projecting from the wall, with a capital and a base) on either side and/or a small Greek pediment (a low triangular gable crowning the doorway) above.

- An odd collection of windows set into the gable ends, glazed with antique glass, is a wonderful quirk of many older Capes. You can replicate this feature by cutting out the windows before you bake the pieces and sprinkling a thin layer of crushed butterscotch candies into the spaces (see page 12). The candy will melt, creating the illusion of old glass.

- A lean-to, which was commonly attached to one side of the house, supported by logs or wooden posts. It would be easy enough to create one out of gingerbread and fill it with pretzel stick or Tootsie Roll firewood.

17. **FINISH THE WINDOWS:** Affix the shutters to the sides of the windows. Use a sharp skewer to poke 3 holes into the long side of each mini Charleston Chew. Insert a 1-inch sprig of thyme into each hole (choose the tough pieces from the bottom of the sprigs, which will remain upright without wilting). Place 2 tablespoons icing in a small bowl and color it pale pink. Fit a pastry bag with the #13 star tip. Pipe a rosette onto each sprig to resemble roses. Dab icing on the back of each window box and attach one box under each window.

18. **CONSTRUCT THE FENCE:** Pipe 2 drops of white icing onto the rounded tops of a pretzel and pipe 1 drop on one side at the pretzel's widest point. Position the pretzel parallel to the house and about 2½ inches from the front of the house, to one side of the door, and glue it, upside down, to the platter or board. Continue to glue the pretzels this way, side by side, all the way around the house, leaving an open space in front of the door.

tip. Fill in random spaces along the foundation with one color. Repeat with the remaining colors so that the ¾-inch strip is entirely covered with stones.

14. **COVER THE CHIMNEY:** Cut the fruit leather to fit the sides of the chimney and glue with icing. Cut twelve ½ x ¼-inch bricks from the remaining fruit leather and glue in a row close to the top of the chimney.

15. **SHINGLE THE ROOF WITH THE TWIZZLERS:** Squeeze a little bit of icing onto the Twizzler pieces, one at a time, and apply a row of Twizzlers along the bottom edge of one side of the roof, interspersing an occasional red piece among the brown and cutting the end pieces to fit where necessary. Apply another row above this one. Continue until you reach the peak of the roof, making about 14 rows in total. Repeat with the other side of the roof.

16. **CONSTRUCT THE ENTRY:** Dab icing on the piece of chocolate and place it in front of the door. Dab icing on the back of the door, place the door on top of the doorstep, and attach it to the house.

DAWSON CITY HOUSE

SEE TEMPLATES ON PAGE 93

INGREDIENTS

1   RECIPE GINGERBREAD
    DOUGH (PAGE 83),
    CHILLED

1   16-OUNCE BAG
    BUTTERSCOTCH
    CANDIES, CRUSHED IN A
    FOOD PROCESSOR

    RED, ORANGE, BLACK,
    GREEN, VIOLET, PINK,
    YELLOW, BLUE, AND
    BROWN FOOD COLORING

2   RECIPES PASTILLAGE
    (PAGE 85)

1/2   CUP FONDANT (SEE
    RESOURCES, PAGE 86)

2   .75-OUNCE POUCHES
    RED FRUIT BY THE FOOT

2   RECIPES ROYAL ICING
    (PAGE 84)

1/2   CUP BRIGHT PINK
    SANDING SUGAR

1   SILVER DRAGÉE

1   2-INCH-LONG PIECE
    THICK BLACK LICORICE

9   GUMMY PENGUINS

Our gold-rush–era house is a simple structure with plain gingerbread sides and back. The front facade, in contrast, is covered with colorful icing and has a DECORATIVELY SHAPED ROOFLINE and prettily piped window casements and door surround. We couldn't resist coating the roof with pink sanding sugar to match the front door for a shiny asphalt look. Because Dawson City is in the Yukon and above the treeline, there are no trees on the landscape. Instead, decorating the area in front of the house is a pastillage Santa driving a sleigh pulled not by dogs or reindeer but rather by gummy penguins.

special equipment

16 X 20-INCH CUTTING BOARD OR FOIL-COVERED STYROFOAM BOARD

PASTRY BAGS AND #44 BASKET-WEAVE TIP, #2 PLAIN TIP, AND #7 PLAIN TIP

CAKE COMB OR SERRATED KNIFE

RIBBON FOR EDGE OF BOARD

CONSTRUCTION NOTES

We decided to make yellow candy glass window panes from crushed butterscotch candy to match our violet and yellow color scheme.

The decorative front of the house is slightly taller than the rear, so we had to glue an extra piece of gingerbread, the same shape as the rear roof peak, to the inside of the front facade in order to support the roof pieces.

Use gel food coloring to achieve the saturated colors.

We named this house after the town at the heart of the Klondike gold rush, although it resembles California gold rush houses as well. In the mid-1890s, Dawson City was a muddy moose pasture where prospectors erected tents and rustic log cabins. The discovery in 1896 of rich veins of gold led to a population stampede as close to 100,000 people descended on the area in hopes of striking it rich. By 1898, nearly 40,000 people were living permanently in the new town. From 1900 to 1903, the prosperity of the gold rush was reflected in more elaborate designs of homes and commercial buildings. The hallmark of the Dawson City house built during this period is a false front with elaborate decorative detailing, which gave the simple wooden building the illusion of affluence and importance.

1. **BAKE THE GINGERBREAD:** Enlarge the templates on pieces of thin cardboard or sturdy paper and cut to size. Preheat the oven to 375°F.

2. Divide the dough into 4 equal pieces. Wrap 3 pieces tightly in plastic wrap and keep in the refrigerator. Lightly flour a piece of parchment paper and roll out the fourth piece of dough onto the parchment so it is ¼ inch thick. Place the template for the front of the house on the dough and cut around the template with a sharp knife. Cut away the door opening and set aside the door piece. Cut away the windows. Remove the scraps from the parchment, wrap them in plastic, and refrigerate.

3. Slide the parchment onto a rimless baking sheet. Place the door piece next to the front piece on the baking sheet, at least 1 inch away from it. Slide the baking sheet into the oven and bake until the door is firm, about 10 minutes. Use a metal spatula to remove the door to a wire rack to cool. Continue to bake the house until the edges are lightly browned and the center is firm, 2 to 4 minutes more. Let the front piece cool on the baking sheet for 5 minutes. Sprinkle crushed candy into each window space, covering the spaces completely with a thin layer, and return the baking sheet to the oven until the candy is melted, 5 to 7 minutes. Remove the pan from the oven again and let the gingerbread cool completely before sliding the piece, still on the parchment, off of the pan.

4. Working in 3 batches and using the remaining 3 pieces of dough plus scraps, repeat the rolling and baking with the rear and 2 side pieces (adding the window glass as before and baking again until melted), roof pieces, and interior roof support pieces.

5. When the pieces are cool, transfer them to baking sheets and tightly cover the sheets in plastic until you are ready to assemble the house. They will keep for up to 1 week.

6. **MAKE THE SANTA AND THE SLEIGH:** Use at least 6 drops food coloring to tint some pastillage bright red, some orange, and some black, leaving some white. Press some red and white pastillage into a greased Santa-shaped candy mold (alternatively, sculpt your Santa freehand) and set aside to dry. Roll out the orange pastillage and shape into a sleigh, wrapping one end around a pencil to mold the small curve at the front of the sleigh and shaping the larger curves against small jars (spice jars work well) or juice glasses. Roll out a strip of black pastillage and cut 2 sleigh blades. Let all the pastillage pieces dry overnight.

7. **MAKE SANTA'S BAG:** Tint the fondant bright green with food coloring. Form into the shape of a bag. Tie with a piece of Fruit by the Foot and set aside to dry overnight.

8. **ICE THE FRONT FACADE:** Cut squares of parchment the same size as the front facade windows and lay them on top of the windows. (The parchment will protect the

windows as you comb the icing.) Use a few drops of food coloring or more if necessary to tint 1½ cups icing violet. Spread a thin layer of the violet icing over the front facade and let stand for 15 minutes. Spread another layer of icing over the first layer, and then use a cake comb or a serrated knife to create the look of siding. Set aside to dry completely, about 3 hours.

9. ICE AND SUGAR THE ROOF PIECES: While the front is drying, spread the sanding sugar in an even layer on a rimmed baking sheet. Tint ¾ cup icing deep pink with 4 drops of food coloring. Cover the roof pieces with the pink-colored icing and then press the pieces, icing side down, into the sanding sugar. Sprinkle sugar over any bald spots. Set aside, icing-side up, to dry completely, at least 1 hour.

10. PIPE THE WINDOW TRIM: While the roof is drying, pipe the window trim. Scrape ½ cup icing into a bowl and color it yellow. Pipe yellow icing, using the plain side of the #44 basket-weave tip, around each window on the front, rear, and side facades. Scrape ½ cup icing

more dawson city style

We kept it simple, but here are a couple of ideas if you want to go further when decorating:

- The false front of the Dawson City House was also standard on commercial buildings, as it allowed for large signs and plate-glass windows. If you'd like, you could make your Dawson City House a commercial building instead: leave off one or all three of the second-story front facade windows and place a sign made of gingerbread with piped lettering on the facade instead. First-story windows could display smaller signs or even drawings of the products sold in the store.

- It is easy to cover the gingerbread door with pink icing and use a basket-weave tip to pipe the panel moldings, but we had fun molding a door with homemade pastillage. If you'd like to try this, use the recipe on page 85, knead in some deep pink food coloring, and mold as follows: Glue 3 cardboard rectangles onto the door template to create 2 small upper panels and 1 large lower panel. Roll out some pastillage, spray nonstick vegetable oil spray on the template, and place the template on top, panel-side down. Press down on the template to make the panel impressions in the pastillage. Use a sharp paring knife to cut around the template. Let the door dry completely, about 24 hours. Attach the doorknob with a drop of icing.

into a small bowl and color bright blue. Use a #2 plain tip to pipe the bright blue icing around the yellow. Let dry for 1 hour.

11. COLOR THE DOOR AND ATTACH THE HARDWARE: While the window trim is drying, smooth pink-colored icing over the door. Fit a pastry bag with the basket-weave tip and scrape the remaining pink icing into the bag. Pipe 2 small upper panels and 1 large lower panel on the door. Press a silver dragée doorknob into the door. Set aside to allow the icing to harden completely, about 1 hour.

12. ASSEMBLE THE HOUSE: Color about 1 cup icing brown if you like, or use plain white icing. Fit a pastry bag with the #7 plain tip and fill with the icing. Keep the rest of the icing in a bowl, pressing a piece of plastic wrap against the surface to prevent it from drying out. If you are illuminating your house, see page 13. Pipe icing along the bottom edge of the front of the house. Position it where you want it to stand on the board and place a heavy mug or can at the back (take care not to damage the decorated front side) to help it stand upright until the icing dries. Pipe icing along the bottom edge and

front edge of one of the sides and attach the side to the front so that the edge of the side is recessed $\frac{1}{2}$ inch from the edge of the front facade. Repeat with the other side and then attach the rear, adding more mugs for support as necessary. Insert straight pins through the side walls into the front wall and through the back wall into each side wall. Wrap the tip of the pastry bag with plastic wrap and refrigerate until you are ready to continue. Let stand until the icing is dry, about 1 hour. Remove the mugs and the pins.

13. ATTACH THE ROOF SUPPORTS: Check the interior roof support pieces to make sure they correspond to the height of the rear facade top; trim with a handheld grater if necessary. Using a little icing, glue the roof supports perpendicular to the inside of the front facade on both sides of the front door. Pin in place and let dry for 15 minutes.

14. PIPE THE MULLIONS: Carefully turn over the front facade piece with the glued-on roof support so the roof support is on the underside. Fit a pastry bag with the #44 basket-weave tip, fill with the blue icing, and pipe a horizontal line and a vertical line across each windowpane. Repeat with the rear facade and the sides. Set the pieces

aside to dry for 1 hour. Remove the pins from the front facade.

15. ATTACH THE ROOF: Pipe icing along the top edges of the sides and along each side edge of one roof piece. Position 1 roof piece on top of the house, lining it up so its top edge runs from the center of the front to the center of the rear of the house, resting the piece on the roof support glued to the inside of the front facade. Secure the roof piece by inserting straight pins through the house and into the roof at the peak and at the eaves. Repeat with the second roof piece. Let stand until the icing is dry, about 1 hour. Remove the pins.

16. ATTACH THE CHIMNEY: Cut one end of the black licorice piece at an angle so it can rest flat but stand straight up on the roof. Glue the licorice piece to the roof.

17. LANDSCAPE THE HOUSE: Cover any exposed board with white icing. Attach the blades to the bottom of the sleigh and let dry for 15 minutes. Glue the sleigh to the board, and then place the Santa behind the sleigh and the bag in the sleigh. Glue gummy penguins to the board with icing and attach them to the sleigh with reins made of Fruit by the Foot.

CARPENTER GOTHIC

SEE TEMPLATES ON PAGE 96

special equipment

16 X 20-INCH CUTTING
BOARD OR FOIL-COVERED
STYROFOAM BOARD

CAKE COMB

PASTRY BAGS AND #2
PLAIN TIP, #7 PLAIN TIP,
#35 STAR TIP, AND #47
BASKET-WEAVE TIP

FONDANT ROLLER,
OPTIONAL

CRAFT SCISSORS

With so much trim and intricacy, this house is an opportunity for people who really love over-the-top seasonal decorating. At the same time, its CHURCHLIKE ROOFLINE, WINDOWS, and DOORS charmingly allude to the holiday.

The effects are not at all difficult to achieve. The BATTEN BOARDS are made of rolled and cut fondant. The SHINGLES on the roof are made from bubble gum cut into 1-inch lengths. The PINNACLES (small upright structures rising above the roof of a building) are formed by piping icing on top of breath mints. Sheet gelatin, which is cross-hatched, stands in as window glass. Other clever details include pieces of red licorice representing the FLUES peeking out of the chimney and more bubble gum by the yard trimmed with a craft scissors to look like BARGE BOARD, the exterior visible flat trim board that follows the slope of the roof.

INGREDIENTS

2 RECIPES GINGER-
BREAD DOUGH (PAGE
83), CHILLED

6 PIECES CLEAR SHEET
GELATIN WITH
CROSS-HATCHING

2 RECIPES ROYAL ICING
(PAGE 84)

PINK, BLUE, RED, AND
BROWN FOOD COLORING

1 SMALL PINK SMARTIES
CANDY

CONFECTIONERS' SUGAR

2 POUNDS FONDANT (SEE
RESOURCES, PAGE 86)

3 SMALL RED GUMDROPS

2 SMALL WHITE GUMDROPS

8 2-OUNCE ROLLS BLUE
BUBBLE TAPE

4 2-OUNCE ROLLS PINK
BUBBLE TAPE

1 CHERRY TWIZZLER

3 PEP-O-MINT LIFE SAVERS

1 RED JELLY RING

1 GREEN JELLY RING

ABOUT 30 GUMMY
SPEARMINT LEAVES
(FROM 2 11-OUNCE
BAGS)

3 MARSHMALLOWS

3 STRIPED RIBBON CANDY
LOLLIPOPS

1 RIBBON CANDY
CHRISTMAS TREE

HISTORICAL NOTE

While they may resemble castles and cathedrals, Carpenter Gothic homes built in the second half of the nineteenth century housed the middle, not upper, classes. The invention of the steam-powered scroll saw in the 1840s allowed for the mass production of the intricate wood trim that is one of the hallmarks of the style. Other identifying features include a steeply pitched roof, batten board (vertical wood) siding, and masonry window trim like the trim on a Gothic cathedral. These details make Carpenter Gothic houses awe-inspiring and whimsical at the same time.

CONSTRUCTION NOTE

The large scale of the house requires that the front and rear facades be baked in two pieces: a large rectangle and a small triangle that will become the pediment. Be sure to let the icing that glues the pediment to the larger piece dry sufficiently before proceeding with construction so the assembled facade will be ready to support the roof and gable pieces.

1. BAKE THE GINGERBREAD: Enlarge the templates on pieces of thin cardboard or sturdy paper and cut to size. Preheat the oven to 375°F.

2. Divide the dough into 6 equal pieces. Wrap 5 pieces tightly in plastic wrap and keep in the refrigerator. Lightly flour a piece of parchment paper and roll out the sixth piece of the dough onto the parchment so it is ¼ inch thick. Place the template for the front of the house on the dough and cut around the template with a sharp knife. Cut away the door opening and set aside the door piece. Cut away the windows. Roll out some of the scraps and cut the chimney, porch facade, and entry porch roof pieces from them. Remove the scraps from the parchment, wrap them in plastic, and refrigerate.

3. Slide the parchment onto a rimless baking sheet. Move the door piece, chimney pieces, and porch pieces to a second sheet of parchment on a separate baking sheet. Slide the baking sheets into the oven. Bake the door, chimney, and porch pieces until firm, about 10 minutes. Continue to bake the front piece until the edges are lightly browned and the center is firm, 2 to 4 minutes more. Slide the parchment onto a wire rack and let cool completely.

4. Working in 5 batches and using the remaining 5 pieces of dough plus scraps, repeat the rolling and baking with the rear, 2 sides, and roof pieces.

5. When the pieces are cool, transfer them to baking sheets and tightly cover the sheets in plastic until you are ready to assemble the house. They will keep for up to 1 week.

6. ATTACH THE WINDOW GLASS: Cut the sheet gelatin pieces in half. Glue 1 piece to the inside of each window with a dab of icing on each corner, for window glass. Let dry for 15 minutes. Turn the gingerbread pieces over so the outsides are facing up on the countertop. Place 3 tablespoons icing in a small bowl and tint with 1 or 2 drops of pink food coloring. Fit a pastry bag with the #2 plain tip, fill with the pink icing, and pipe diagonal lines across each window, following the lines on the gelatin. Let dry for 15 minutes.

7. ICE THE DOOR: Place ¼ cup icing in a small bowl and tint with a few drops of blue food coloring. Use a small offset spatula to ice the door piece with the blue icing. Use a cake comb to score the icing vertically. Press the Smarties candy into the icing as a doorknob. Set aside to dry for at least 2 hours.

With the Carpenter Gothic, there's no such thing as too much decoration. To further embellish your house, consider adding one or more of the following elements:

- Decorative stained-glass centerfoil window: To create this effect, substitute candy glass windows (see page 12 for instructions) for the clear gelatin.

- Elaborate bay windows: You can build a bay window into the rear facade using gingerbread and sheet gelatin, or draw one on with colored icing.

- A one-story porch with carved porch railings: Construct one along the rear facade on either side of the bay window.

8. **ROLL OUT, CUT, AND ATTACH THE FONDANT BATTEN BOARDS:** Lightly dust the countertop with confectioners' sugar. Knead a few drops of red food coloring and 1 or 2 drops of brown into the fondant until it is an oxblood red. Cut it into 3 equal pieces and tightly wrap 2 of the pieces in plastic wrap. Roll the third piece into a large rectangle measuring at least 12 inches across and $\frac{1}{8}$ inch thick. Cut the fondant into 12 x 1-inch strips using a fondant roller. Attach strips of fondant vertically to the front, rear, and sides of the house with icing, cutting them to fit around the windows and leaving about $\frac{1}{16}$ inch of gingerbread peeking between each piece of batten board. Pipe a thin line of icing between each strip. Let dry for 15 minutes.

9. **ASSEMBLE THE HOUSE:** If you are illuminating your house, see page 13 for instructions. Fit a pastry bag with the #7 plain tip and fill with icing. Keep the rest of the icing in a bowl, pressing a piece of plastic wrap against the surface to prevent it from drying out. Pipe icing on the long sides of the chimney pieces and glue them together

to create a rectangular box, standing them vertically and upside down until dry.

10. Pipe icing along the bottom edge of the front of the house. Position it where you want it to stand on the board and place a heavy mug or can on each side to help it stand upright until the icing dries. Pipe icing along the bottom edge and front edge of one of the sides and attach the side to the front so that the side edge of the side piece is flush against the back of the front piece. Repeat with the other side piece and the rear, adding more mugs for support as necessary. Insert straight pins through the front wall into each side wall and through the back wall into each side wall.

11. **ATTACH THE LARGE ROOF:** Pipe icing along the top edges of the sides and along each side edge of 1 of the 4 A pieces. Position the roof piece on top of the house, lining it up so its top edge runs with the tip of piece A at the center of the roof and the other edges creating the eaves. Secure the roof piece by inserting straight pins through the front and back of the house and into the roof at the peak and at the eaves. Repeat with the second roof piece. Install the 2 remaining large roof pieces A following the same procedure. Wrap the tip of the pastry bag with plastic wrap and refrigerate until you are ready to continue. Let stand until the icing is dry, about 1 hour. Remove the pins.

12. **ATTACH THE SMALL ROOF GABLES:** Pipe icing along the bottom, back, and top edges of 2 gable pieces (B). To create the front gable, position them on top of the house so they come together at the top and fit flush into the roof. Repeat with the remaining 2 gable pieces (B) to create the rear gable.

13. **CONSTRUCT THE ENTRYWAY:** Pipe icing on the back of the door, near the edge.

Glue it to the doorway. Pipe icing along the longest straight edges of pieces C and D and attach them to either side of the doorway. Pipe icing along the front edges of pieces C and D and attach piece E. Pipe icing along the top edges of the entry walls and glue on the roof. Pipe a little icing onto each small gumdrop and arrange the gumdrops in a row on top of the entryway roof, alternating red and white.

14. SHINGLE THE ROOF WITH THE BUBBLE GUM: Cut the blue gum into 1-inch lengths. Squeeze a little bit of icing on the gum pieces, one at a time, and apply a row of gum pieces along the bottom edge of one side of the roof. Apply another row above this one, slightly overlapping it. Continue until you reach the peak of the roof, making 17 or 18 rows in total. Repeat with the other side of the roof.

15. SHINGLE THE GABLES: Cut 1 of the pink bubble gum lengths into 1-inch pieces. Shingle the gables, alternating pink and blue rows of gum and cutting the gum pieces to fit as necessary.

16. ATTACH THE SCROLLWORK: Use craft scissors to make a scalloped edge along one side of the remaining pink bubble gum length. Cut the pieces to fit the roof edges and attach them with a thin line of icing piped along the back top edge of the gum.

17. ATTACH THE CHIMNEY: Squeeze a thin line of icing along the bottom edges of the chimney and attach it at the peak of the left side of the roof. Cut the Twizzler in half and squeeze a thin line of icing along one side of each piece. Carefully insert the pieces into the chimney side by side so that they protrude about 2 inches.

18. TRIM THE CHIMNEY, DOORWAY, ROOF, AND SIDING: Fit a pastry bag with the #2 plain tip, fill with some icing, and pipe lines resembling bricks on all sides of the chimney. Pipe a thin line of icing around the outside edge of the entryway. Pipe a thin line of icing along the roof joints and on the edges where the scrollwork meets the shingles.

19. ATTACH THE PINNACLES: Squeeze a little bit of icing onto a Life Saver and place it at the center point of the roof. Fit a pastry bag with the #35 star tip. Stir a tablespoon or two of confectioners' sugar into $\frac{1}{4}$ cup icing to stiffen it. Fill the pastry bag with the icing. Place the tip on the Life Saver. Squeeze and pull to create a large $2\frac{1}{2}$-inch pinnacle. Repeat on each end of the roof with the remaining 2 Life Savers, making smaller $1\frac{1}{2}$-inch pinnacles.

20. TRIM THE WINDOWS: Fit a pastry bag with the #47 basket-weave tip and fill with icing. Pipe icing around each window.

21. Use a sharp paring knife to cut a few thin strips from the red jelly ring. Shape into a ribbon and glue to the green jelly ring. Attach the jelly ring wreath to the house above the center front window.

22. LANDSCAPE THE HOUSE: Use a large offset spatula to spread a thin layer of icing in front of the house and to the edge of the board, to resemble a snow-covered yard. Stand the spearmint leaves upright all along the front and sides of the house, securing them by pushing them into the icing. Place the marshmallows in a group to one side of the front of the house, gluing them to the board with icing. Trim the lollipop sticks to the desired lengths and insert into the marshmallows, securing them also to the sides of the house and/or the roof edges with icing. Place the ribbon candy Christmas tree

on top of the icing at the other end of the front of the house.

GREEK REVIVAL ANTEBELLUM PLANTATION

Our house has a SYMMETRICAL plan. Its large and evenly spaced windows have bold but simple moldings. It has an ENTRY PORCH with columns made of stacked peppermint candies and a PEDIMENTED GABLE (the triangular portion of the front or side of a building enclosed by or masking the end of a pitched roof) with a CRENELLATED FRIEZE (the notched band running above the columns). The white CLAPBOARD SIDING is typical of the style; Greek Revival houses were always painted white because it was not commonly known until later in the century that the white marble of the original Greek structures was in many cases COLORFULLY PAINTED.

INGREDIENTS

1½ RECIPES GINGER-BREAD DOUGH (PAGE 83), CHILLED

2½ RECIPES ROYAL ICING (PAGE 84)

64 STARLIGHT MINTS (FROM 2 1-POUND BAGS)

1 ICE CREAM SUGAR CONE

55 SOUR PATCH GREEN APPLE GUMMY CANDIES (ABOUT 5 OUNCES)

27 STICKS JUICY FRUIT GUM (FROM 2 2¼-OUNCE PACKAGES)

1 STICK WRIGLEY'S SPEARMINT GUM

BLACK, BROWN, AND RED FOOD COLORING

2 YELLOW M&MS

23 PIECES EXTRA GREEN APPLE GUM (FROM 2 2¼-OUNCE PACKAGES)

8 RED LICORICE WHEELS (SELECT THE FLATTEST WHEELS)

ABOUT 40 PIECES PINK BAZOOKA BUBBLE GUM (FROM 2 4-OUNCE BOXES)

5 RED SOUR POWER BELTS (ABOUT 1½ OUNCES)

10 .81-OUNCE PACKAGES OREO THIN CRISPS (ABOUT 200 COOKIES)

CONSTRUCTION NOTE

Don't worry if your starlight mint columns look a little wobbly. They will give the house a charmingly decayed look. But if you prefer ramrod straight columns, you can use striped ribbon candy lollipops, cut to measure with a serrated knife, instead.

special equipment

16 x 20-INCH CUTTING BOARD OR FOIL-COVERED STYROFOAM BOARD

PASTRY BAGS AND #7 PLAIN TIP AND #47 BASKET-WEAVE TIP

CRAFT SCISSORS

In the early nineteenth century, British architectural styles fell out of favor as newly independent Americans cultivated an interest in ancient Greece. Taking Greek temples as symbols of the democratic ideal, civic leaders in Philadelphia, Washington, D.C., and other U.S. cities commissioned public buildings in the style, and soon the trend made its way into domestic architecture through the architectural pattern books published at the time. Such houses, many rather grand, sprang up in the American South; they will be forever associated with the pre–Civil War period through images of Tara, the fictional mansion in the MGM blockbuster *Gone With the Wind*.

more greek revival style

The simple, stately appearance of the Greek Revival could be enhanced by the following architectural and landscape elements:

- Porches and balconies: Common to this style, either or both could be added to the sides of the house to make it more grand.

- Domed skylights, which illuminate the interior of some plantations. Advanced gingerbread architects might consider adding one here.

- A low stone fence (made from chocolate pebbles).

1. BAKE THE GINGERBREAD: Enlarge the templates on pieces of thin cardboard or sturdy paper and cut to size. Preheat the oven to 375°F.

2. Divide the dough into 6 equal pieces. Wrap 5 pieces tightly in plastic wrap and keep in the refrigerator. Lightly flour a piece of parchment paper and roll out the sixth piece of the dough onto the parchment so it is ¼ inch thick. Place the template for the front of the house on the dough and cut around the template with a sharp knife. Cut away the door opening, cut the door piece into 2 equal rectangles (these will be the double front doors), and set aside. Cut away the windows. Remove the scraps from the parchment, wrap them in plastic, and refrigerate.

3. Slide the parchment onto a rimless baking sheet. Place the door pieces next to the front piece on the baking sheet, at least 1 inch away from it. Slide the baking sheet into the oven and bake until the door is firm, about 10 minutes. Use a metal spatula to remove the door to a wire rack to cool. Continue to bake the house until the edges are lightly browned and the center is firm, 2 to 4 minutes more. Slide the parchment onto a wire rack and let cool completely.

4. Working in 5 batches and using the remaining 5 pieces of dough plus scraps, repeat the rolling and baking with the rear, 2 sides, roof, pediment, and chimney pieces. Use gingerbread dough that has been rolled out a couple of times for the front pediment; this dough will not puff up as much.

5. When the pieces are cool, transfer them to baking sheets and tightly cover the sheets in plastic until you are ready to assemble the house. They will keep for up to 1 week.

6. MAKE THE COLUMNS: On a parchment-lined rimmed baking sheet, use icing to glue together the centers of 12 or 13 starlight mints, using the edge of the pan as a guide, to form one column. Repeat with enough mints to create 4 columns in total. (You will add 2 to 3 more mints to the top of each column when placing the columns in the final position.) Straighten the columns against the edge of the baking sheet with a full box of confectioners' sugar pressed against the exposed edge of the mint column. Let the columns rest until completely dry, at least 6 hours.

7. MAKE THE TREE AND ANGEL: Stand the ice cream cone upside down on the baking sheet holding the columns. Pipe small dots of icing on the backs of the gummy sour apple candies and glue them to the ice cream cone to cover it completely. Use a sharp paring knife to cut out the angel's wings from a piece of Juicy Fruit gum. Cut out the angel's body from the Wrigley's Spearmint gum. Pipe a dot of icing onto the wing piece and glue it to the back of the body piece. Pipe a small dot of icing on top of the tree and stand the angel on the icing.

8. MAKE THE MULLIONED WINDOWS: Use a sharp chef's knife to cut the remaining pieces of Juicy Fruit gum lengthwise into 5 strips each. Use icing to glue the strips on the inside of the side, front, and back pieces so they crisscross the windows, 2 going lengthwise and then 3 going crosswise. Set aside to dry for 15 minutes.

9. ICE THE DOORS AND ATTACH THE DOORKNOBS: Fill a small bowl with 3 tablespoons icing and tint with a few drops of black food coloring. Smooth a thin layer of icing over each door piece. Transfer the remaining icing to a pastry bag fitted with the

#47 basket-weave tip and use the smooth side to pipe 2 boxes on each door to create the panels. Place an M&M doorknob on each door. Let stand to dry for at least 2 hours.

10. ASSEMBLE THE HOUSE: If you are illuminating your house, see page 13. Fit a pastry bag with the #7 plain tip and fill with icing. Keep the rest of the icing in a bowl, pressing a piece of plastic wrap against the surface to prevent it from drying out. Pipe icing along the bottom edge of the rear of the house. Position it where you want it to stand on the board and place a heavy mug or can on each side to help it stand upright until the icing dries. Pipe icing along the bottom edge and rear edge of one of the sides and attach the side to the back so the side edge of the side piece is flush against the front of the back piece. Repeat with the other side, adding more mugs for support as necessary. Insert straight pins through the back wall into each side wall. Pipe icing along the bottom edge of the front of the house and attach it to the sides so the front edges are flush with the longer edges of the side pieces. Wrap the tip of the pastry bag with plastic wrap and refrigerate until you are ready to continue. Let stand until the icing is dry, about 1 hour. Remove the mugs and pins.

11. ATTACH THE ROOF: Pipe icing along the top edges of the sides and along each side edge of 1 roof piece. Position the roof piece on top of the house, lining it up so its top edge runs from front to back of the house. Secure the roof piece by inserting straight pins through the front and back of the house and into the roof at the peak and at the eaves. Repeat with the second roof piece. Let stand until the icing is dry, about 1 hour. Remove the pins.

12. ICE THE HOUSE AND CREATE THE SIDING: Use a small offset spatula to smooth a thin layer of white icing over the back wall of the house and around the windows. Drag a ruler or other straightedge across the icing horizontally, making lines about ¾ inch apart, to create the siding, wiping the ruler with a paper towel after each line. Repeat with the sides and front of the house.

13. PIPE THE WINDOW TRIM: Fit a pastry bag with the #47 basket-weave tip. Add some icing and use the smooth side of the tip to pipe around each window to create the trim.

14. ATTACH THE SHUTTERS: Use a sharp paring knife to cut each piece of green apple gum lengthwise. With the pastry bag fitted with the #7 plain tip, pipe a line of icing down each piece of gum and attach on each side of each window.

15. LAY DOWN THE FRONT PAVING STONES AND LOWER CAPITAL: Use a small offset spatula to spread a thin layer of icing on the board in front of and all around the house. Arrange 4 of the licorice wheels in a row in front of the house, in line with the narrow pieces extending from the house (the columns will rest on these pieces and support the pediment and frieze, to be attached later). Arrange the bubble gum pieces in rows in front of the house, cutting them to fit around

the licorice wheels, to create the paving-stone porch. Let stand until the icing on the board is dry, about 1 hour.

16. ATTACH THE DOORS: Pipe icing onto the back of the front door pieces, near the edges. Glue the doorpieces to the doorway so they are resting on top of the bubble gum. Glue the back door in place.

17. POSITION THE CAPITALS AND COLUMNS: Place the center 2 columns so they frame the front entry door. Pipe icing onto the 4 flat licorice wheels in front of the house and carefully stand the columns on them. Pipe icing onto the top of the mint columns and one by one add a mint to the top of each column until the column—plus a final top licorice wheel (the capital)—supports the frieze. Place a small drinking glass next to each column to support it while it dries, about 1 hour.

18. ATTACH THE PEDIMENT: Pipe icing onto the front edges of the roof and onto the licorice capitals. Glue the pediment to the roof, resting it on the capitals. Secure with straight pins inserted into the roof. Let stand until the icing is dry, about 1 hour. Remove the pins.

19. ICE AND DECORATE THE PEDIMENT AND FRIEZE: Use craft scissors to trim the edges of 3 of the Sour Power Belts decoratively. Cut 2 of them into 6-inch lengths and 1 into an 11-inch length. These pieces will form the exterior triangle decoration on the pediment. Leave the edges of the other 2 fruit strips straight and cut them to get 2 lengths measuring 3½ inches and 1 measuring 6 inches. These will form the interior decoration. Use a small offset spatula to spread a layer of icing all over the pediment. With the pastry bag fitted with the #47 basket-weave tip and, using the striped side, pipe up and down along each cutout section of the frieze.

20. ATTACH THE CHIMNEYS: Pipe icing along the long sides of one set of chimney pieces and glue them together to make a rectangular box. Attach the chimney to the left side of the roof between the first and second windows. Repeat with the second set of chimney pieces.

21. ICE THE CHIMNEYS: Fill a small bowl with ⅓ cup icing and tint with brown food coloring and a little red to achieve a brick red. Smooth a thin layer of icing over each chimney.

22. SHINGLE THE ROOF: Squeeze a little bit of icing on the Oreo Crisps, one at a time, and apply in a row along the bottom edge of the side of the roof without the chimneys. Apply another row above the first and slightly overlapping it. Continue until you reach the peak of the roof, making 8 rows in total. Repeat with the chimney side, breaking the cookies to fit into the space between the chimneys as necessary.

VICTORIAN FARMHOUSE

SEE TEMPLATES ON PAGE 105

special equipment

16 x 20-INCH CUTTING BOARD OR FOIL-COVERED STYROFOAM BOARD

PASTRY BAGS AND # 2 PLAIN TIP, #7 PLAIN TIP, #47 BASKET-WEAVE TIP, #4 PLAIN TIP, AND #3 ROUND TIP

To distinguish our Victorian gingerbread house from the Carpenter Gothic and the Second Empire (both of which are also from the Victorian period), we made it less formal and more rural, more of a farmhouse than a town house. The HIGH-PITCHED ROOF, ASYMMETRICAL LAYOUT, and VERANDA with a pressed tin roof are all typical Victorian farmhouse features.

HISTORICAL NOTE

"Victorian" describes not really a decorative style but the period of the English queen Victoria's reign (1837 to 1901). The era encompasses a variety of styles, including Gothic Revival, Italianate, Second Empire, Queen Anne, and Shingle, that became popular in the United States. Builders of the time often incorporated elements from several styles, and the quirky results became known as Victorian.

INGREDIENTS

2 RECIPES GINGER-BREAD DOUGH (PAGE 83), CHILLED

½ CUP (ABOUT 2½ OUNCES) RED HARD CANDIES, CRUSHED IN A FOOD PROCESSOR

1 16-OUNCE BAG CARAMEL-COLORED OR CLEAR HARD CANDIES, CRUSHED IN A FOOD PROCESSOR

5 SHEETS EDIBLE RICE PAPER (SEE RESOURCES, PAGE 86)

2 RECIPES ROYAL ICING (PAGE 84)

GREEN, VIOLET, HOLIDAY RED, BROWN, AND ORANGE FOOD COLORING

3 STRIPED CANDY STICKS

50 STICKS LICORICE-FLAVORED GUM, SUCH AS BLACK JACK (FROM 10 5-STICK PACKS)

1 14-OUNCE BAG GREEN WILTON CANDY MELTS

2 POUNDS FONDANT (SEE RESOURCES, PAGE 86)

3 PEPPERMINT-STRIPED CANDY BALLS

3 SMALL RED JUJUBES

3 OBLONG SILVER DRAGÉES

PURPLE, BROWN, GRAY, AND WHITE NECCO WAFERS (FROM 2 2.02-OUNCE PACKAGES)

1 BLACK HARIBO RASPBERRY CANDY

1 BLACK LICORICE LACE

1 .74-OUNCE POUCH RED FRUIT BY THE FOOT

⅓ CUP EDIBLE GREEN GLITTER (SEE RESOURCES, PAGE 86)

1 RECIPE GREEN RICE KRISPIE TREATS (PAGE 44), WARM FROM THE POT

2 TEASPOONS SMALL COLORED DRAGÉES

20 RED SUGAR HEART DECORATIONS

CONSTRUCTION NOTES

The house is basically two boxes that when joined, make a rather large structure. The first time we built this one, we thought we could save time by leaving out the interior wall between the two boxes, as it wouldn't be seen, but the resulting house wasn't as structurally sound as we would have liked; the exterior walls sagged slightly in the middle. Next time we added that wall, assembling first one box and then another, and the house stood up straight and tall for months.

The shingles were another issue. We loved the look of colored chocolate, melted and then cut into shingle shapes. But we found that covering the entire roof

with the shingles wasn't a good idea. The chocolate contains so much oil and moisture that it eventually softens the roof pieces. The solution was to just edge the roof with a few rows of Candy Melt shingles, and then cover the rest of the roof with a smooth sheet of fondant, which looks like freshly fallen snow. (To simplify, you can spread Royal Icing on the roof and lawn instead of using fondant.)

Edible rice paper (available at baking supply stores and by mail) can be cut to resemble drapes. In a pinch you can substitute parchment paper (which is not edible) for the rice paper.

1. **BAKE THE GINGERBREAD:** Enlarge the templates on pieces of thin cardboard or sturdy paper and cut to size. Preheat the oven to 375°F.

2. Divide the dough into 6 equal pieces. Wrap 5 pieces tightly in plastic wrap and keep in the refrigerator. Lightly flour a piece of parchment paper and roll out the sixth piece of the dough onto the parchment so it is ¼ inch thick. Place the template for front piece *F* on the dough and cut around the template with a sharp knife. Cut away the windows. Remove the scraps from the parchment, wrap them in plastic, and refrigerate.

3. Slide the parchment onto a rimless baking sheet. Slide the baking sheet into the oven and bake until the edges are lightly browned and the center is firm, 12 to 14 minutes. Remove from the oven and let cool on the pan for 5 minutes. Sprinkle red crushed candy into the round window space and caramel-colored candy into the remaining window spaces, covering the spaces completely with a thin layer, and return the baking sheet to the oven until the candy is melted, 5 to 7 minutes. Remove the pan from the oven and let the gingerbread cool completely before sliding the gingerbread, still on the parchment, off the pan and continuing.

4. Working in 4 batches and using 4 of the remaining pieces of dough plus scraps, repeat the rolling and baking with the remaining front piece *A*, the rear piece *C*, the interior wall piece *D*, and the 2 side pieces *B* and *E*, adding window glass as before and baking again until melted.

5. Roll out the remaining dough piece along with the scraps and cut the roof pieces, chimney pieces, veranda pieces, and front doorstep pieces. Roll out 2 extra rectangles, one about the length of the narrow portion of the front facade and one about the length of the wider portion of the front facade and a couple of inches deep (these will sit under the fondant snow to make the sloping lawn). Bake until the edges are lightly browned and the center is firm, about 10 minutes for the door and chimney pieces, and 12 to 14 minutes for the rest. Slide the pieces, still on the parchment, onto wire racks to cool completely.

6. When the pieces are cool, transfer them to baking sheets and tightly cover the sheets in plastic until ready to assemble. They will keep for up to 1 week.

7. **ATTACH THE DRAPES:** Cut the rice paper into drapery shapes and use white icing to attach the drapes to the insides of the windows.

8. **COLOR THE VERANDA ROOF:** Scrape ½ cup icing into a small bowl and use a few drops of green food coloring to tint it bright green. Smooth a thin layer of icing over the veranda roof. Cover the remaining green icing with plastic wrap and set aside. Scrape ⅔ cup icing into a small bowl and use a few drops of food coloring to tint it bright violet. Fit a pastry bag with the #2 plain tip, add the violet icing, and pipe violet lines on top of the green to create the pressed tin roof. Let stand to dry for at least 2 hours.

9. **PIPE THE MULLIONS:** Use the violet icing and the #2 tip to pipe mullions—one vertical line and one horizontal line—onto the candy windows on the front and side pieces, excepting the round center window.

10. **PIPE THE DECORATIVE ROUND TRIM AND COLOR THE DOOR:** Fit a

pastry bag with the #7 plain tip and trim the front and back round center windows. Spread violet icing on the door with a small metal spatula. Let stand to dry for at least 2 hours.

11. PIPE THE WINDOW AND DOOR TRIM: Place ½ cup icing in a small bowl and use at least 6 drops of food coloring to tint the icing red. Scrape the icing into a pastry bag fitted with the #47 basket-weave tip and use the plain side to pipe around each window and around the doorway. Let stand to dry for about 1 hour.

12. ASSEMBLE THE HOUSE: If you are illuminating your house, see page 13. Color about 1 cup icing brown, if you like, or use plain white icing. Fit a pastry bag with the #7 tip and fill with the

icing. Pipe icing along the bottom edge of piece A. Position it where you want it to stand on the board and place a heavy mug or can on each side to help it stand upright until the icing dries. Pipe icing along the bottom edge and front edge of piece B and attach to the front so that the side edge of the side piece is flush against the back of the front piece. Repeat with the rear piece C, adding more mugs for support as necessary. Attach piece D by piping icing along the bottom edge and back edge, and along the dotted line indicated on the template. Glue piece D flush with the rear, and glue the front facade piece A to piece D at the dotted line. Insert straight pins through the front wall into each side wall and through the back wall into each side wall.

13. Pipe icing along the bottom and side edges of piece E and attach it to the back piece. Pipe icing along the bottom and side edges of piece F and attach to the sides of pieces E and D so the back edge of the front piece is flush against the side edge of the side wall piece. Secure with straight pins. Wrap the tip of the pastry bag with plastic wrap and refrigerate until ready to continue. Let stand until the

more victorian style

For the pleasingly hodgepodge Victorian look, you could add any combination of the following:

• Lacy gingerbread trim similar to that shown on the Carpenter Gothic (page 29).

• Ornamental stickwork (half-timbers made from Twizzlers and filled in with masonry icing, as on the Tudor Revival, page 64) suggesting medieval building techniques, as used on stick-style Victorian houses.

• A tower, turret, or wraparound porch.

icing is dry, about 1 hour. Remove the mugs and pins.

14. ATTACH THE ROOF: Pipe icing along the top edges of the sides and along each side edge of large roof piece G. Position the roof piece on top of the left side of the house, lining it up so its top edge runs from the front piece to the rear piece. Secure piece G by inserting a straight pin through the roof and into the front and back of the house at the eaves. Repeat with piece H. Let stand until the icing is dry, about 1 hour. Remove the pins. Repeat with pieces I and J on the shorter section of the house, lining it up so that its top edge runs from the point where the roof-lines meet to the gable end.

15. CONSTRUCT THE VERANDA: Pipe icing on

Green Rice Krispie Treats

Rice Krispie Treats, dyed green, can be molded into pretty trees, shrubs, and neat hedges and rolled in green edible glitter if you like. Use this recipe (adapted from the back of the cereal box) to make the trees for the Victorian Farmhouse and to landscape other houses in this book.

MAKES 3½ CUPS

1½ TABLESPOONS VEGETABLE SHORTENING	GREEN FOOD COLORING
20 REGULAR MARSHMALLOWS OR 2 CUPS MINIATURE MARSHMALLOWS	3 CUPS RICE KRISPIES OR OTHER TOASTED RICE CEREAL

In a large saucepan, combine the shortening and marshmallows and cook over low heat, stirring, until the marshmallows are completely melted and the mixture is smooth. Stir in green food coloring drop by drop to achieve the color you want for your trees. Stir in the Rice Krispies until well coated. Use the mixture immediately.

the edges of the veranda deck support pieces. Attach one short piece to the left side of the deck so that it is flush with the wall. Attach the end of the second short piece at the corner of the front and side pieces. Attach the long piece to the front ends of the small supports. Glue the veranda deck to the support pieces. Let dry for 1 hour.

16. Check the height and placement of the veranda roof and then cut the candy sticks to form supports. Cut 2½ inches from each candy stick with a serrated knife. Working with the veranda roof and the candy sticks at the same time, use icing to glue the sticks to the veranda floor and rest the roof on top of them, gluing it to the sticks and to the front of the house. Glue the steps to the board in front of the house. Let stand to dry for 1 hour.

17. PIPE THE VERANDA RAILINGS: Fit a pastry bag with the #4 plain tip, add violet icing, and pipe the veranda railings onto a piece of parchment paper, making a few extras in case some break. Let dry completely, about 4 hours or overnight. Glue the veranda railings to the candy stick columns.

18. ASSEMBLE, BRICK, AND ATTACH THE CHIMNEY: Pipe icing on the long sides of the above roof chimney pieces and glue them together to make a rectangle box, standing them vertically and upside down until dry. Pipe icing on the long sides of the below roof chimney pieces and glue the side pieces to the front piece. Set aside until dry. Cut the licorice gum into ½ x ¼-inch pieces. Smooth white icing over the chimney and press the gum pieces into the icing in a staggered pattern to resemble brick, cutting them as necessary to fit. Pipe icing along the back sides of the under roof chimney piece and attach to the left side wall as indicated on the template. Attach the above roof chimney piece to the roof above the larger chimney piece.

19. SHINGLE THE ROOF: Line a rimmed baking sheet with parchment paper. Place the Candy Melts in a microwave-safe bowl and microwave on high until just melted. Whisk until smooth. Use a thin metal spatula to spread the mixture over the parchment to a ⅛-inch thickness. Run the spatula back and forth, perpendicular to the length of the pan; this will create the texture of slate roof shingles. Let the candy stand until almost set but still soft, about 12 minutes, and use a sharp paring knife to score it into 1-inch-square pieces. Let stand to set completely, 1 to 2 hours.

20. When placing the green roof shingles, keep in mind that the direction of the slate or wood texture should run from the peak of the roof to the eave; in real life that direction would facilitate water runoff. Squeeze a little bit of

white icing on the shingles, one at a time, and apply a row of shingles along the bottom edge of one side of the roof. Apply another row above this one, slightly overlapping it. Repeat with 1 or 2 more rows. Repeat with all sides of the roof. Let stand to dry for 1 hour.

21. ATTACH THE FONDANT SNOW AND PIPE THE ICICLES: Roll half of the fondant to a 1/4-inch thickness, wrapping the remaining fondant tightly in plastic. Spread a thin layer of icing over the parts of the roof that aren't covered with shingles. Place one layer of fondant over the roof, pressing it into the icing but keeping the fondant on the inside of the roof shingles. Drape a second layer of fondant onto the roof, this time overlapping the shingles. Use scissors to trim its edges, leaving the roof covered but the shingles exposed. Using a pastry bag fitted with a #3 round tip and white icing, pipe icicles from the roof areas where the white fondant overlaps

the eaves. Carefully cover the wall areas with parchment paper to prevent icing from dripping onto the house.

22. MAKE THE PINNACLES: Glue the peppermint-striped candy balls to the 3 ends of the roof with white icing. Use a skewer to make a depression in each Jujube and insert an oblong dragée. Glue the Jujubes to the candy balls.

23. LANDSCAPE THE HOUSE: Glue the gingerbread lawn pieces to the board in front of the house on each side of the stairs. Reserve 1 cup fondant, wrapping it well in plastic. Roll out the remaining fondant and cut it to fit around the house, draping it over the ginger-bread pieces to create a sloping front yard. Break the Necco wafers into pieces and glue them to the fondant with white icing to make a walkway.

24. MAKE THE SNOWMAN: Tint a tiny piece of fondant with a drop of orange food coloring. Roll the remaining fondant into 3 balls of decreasing size and glue them together with white icing. Glue a black raspberry candy on the head. Insert black licorice arms into the body and press black licorice pieces into the head to make eyes and a mouth. Shape the orange fondant piece into a cone and attach as the nose. Cut a strip of Fruit by the Foot to make a scarf for the snowman. Attach the snowman to the front lawn.

25. MAKE THE RICE KRISPIE TREAT TREES: Spread the green glitter on the bottom of a rimmed baking sheet. Scrape one third of the Rice Krispies mixture onto a piece of parchment paper. Roll it into a cone shape using the parchment as a guide, and then roll the still-tacky tree in the glitter. Repeat twice to make 2 more trees. Glue the trees to the board. Press colored dragées on one and hearts on another. Cut a piece of Fruit by the Foot and wrap around the third.

SECOND EMPIRE HOUSE

SEE TEMPLATES ON PAGE 111

Authentic details of this style translate beautifully into gingerbread. Our house has a projecting PORTICO entrance (a roof supported by columns or PIERS, usually attached to a building as a porch), tall first-story windows, decorative METALWORK made with piped icing at the rooftop, and dentils (small, closely spaced blocks often used in classical architecture beneath cornices) at the underside of the eaves made of small pacifier-shaped candies. And of course, it has the hallmark double-sloping MANSARD ROOF.

INGREDIENTS

2 RECIPES GINGERBREAD DOUGH (PAGE 83), CHILLED

1 16-OUNCE BAG BUTTERSCOTCH OR CLEAR HARD CANDIES, CRUSHED IN A FOOD PROCESSOR

1 RECIPE ROYAL ICING (PAGE 84)

VIOLET, PINK, BROWN, IVORY, AND BRIGHT GREEN FOOD COLORING

2 ROUND SILVER DRAGÉES

ABOUT 30 TINY PACIFIER-SHAPED CANDIES IN ASSORTED COLORS (ABOUT 1 OUNCE)

1 2-GRAM CONTAINER EDIBLE GOLD LUSTER DUST (SEE RESOURCES, PAGE 86)

¼ CUP CLEAR EDIBLE ALCOHOL, SUCH AS POIRE WILLIAM OR VODKA

2 STRIPED CANDY STICKS

2 SMALL LOG-SHAPED PIECES BAZOOKA BUBBLE GUM

2 SMALL ROUND GUM BALLS

1 3-OUNCE PACKAGE AIRHEAD EXTREMES SOUR BELTS

38 BLUE-AND-AQUA-STRIPED SOUR POWER BELTS (ABOUT 12 OUNCES)

20 KRAFT CARAMELS

1 THICK RED TWIZZLER

1 CUP SWEETENED FLAKED COCONUT

8 WATERMELON GUM BALLS

4 SMALL (4-INCH) PRETZEL STICKS

4 ROLO CHOCOLATE-AND-CARAMEL CANDIES

special equipment

16 X 20-INCH CUTTING BOARD OR FOIL-COVERED STYROFOAM BOARD

PASTRY BAGS AND #2 PLAIN TIP, #47 BASKETWEAVE TIP, #7 PLAIN TIP, #45 PLAIN TIP, AND #3 PLAIN TIP

ELECTRIC DRILL OR HAMMER AND SMALL NAIL

HISTORICAL NOTE

Second Empire homes (also called Mansard after the architect François Mansart, who popularized the style in France), built between 1855 and 1885, show the influence of the extravagant architecture of Paris during the reign of Napoléon III. Their height, a hallmark of the style, originally served a practical purpose, allowing for maximum living space in houses originally built on narrow city lots.

To support the roof (really two roofs), we rested a flat piece of gingerbread on top of the four walls and built the roof on top of that. In addition, a piece of gingerbread placed inside the house gives extra support to prevent the roof from bowing inward.

PROCEDURE

1. **BAKE THE GINGERBREAD:** Enlarge the templates on pieces of thin cardboard or sturdy paper and cut to size. Preheat the oven to 375°F.

2. Divide the dough into 8 equal pieces. Wrap 7 pieces tightly in plastic wrap and keep in the refrigerator. Lightly flour a piece of parchment paper and roll out the eighth piece of dough onto the parchment so it is ¼ inch thick. Place the template for the front of the house on the dough and cut around the template with a sharp knife. Cut away the door opening. Cut away the windows. Remove the scraps from the parchment, wrap them in plastic, and refrigerate.

3. Slide the parchment onto a rimless baking sheet. Slide the baking sheet into the oven and bake until the edges are lightly browned and the center is firm, 12 to 14 minutes. Remove from the oven and let cool on the pan for 5 minutes.

4. Sprinkle crushed hard candy into the window spaces and door space, covering the spaces completely with a thin layer, and return the baking sheet to the oven until the candy is melted, 5 to 7 minutes. Remove the pan from the oven again and let the gingerbread cool completely before sliding the pieces, still on the parchment, off the pan and continuing.

5. Working in 4 batches and using 4 of the remaining pieces of dough plus scraps, repeat the rolling and baking with the front entry, rear, interior support pieces, roof supports, and 2 side pieces, adding window glass as before and baking again until melted.

6. Roll out the remaining 3 dough pieces and cut all roof pieces, the high foundation pieces, front entry sides, portico, and stair pieces. Bake in 3 batches.

7. When the pieces are cool, transfer them to baking sheets and tightly cover the sheets in plastic until you are ready to assemble the house. They will keep for up to 1 week.

8. **PIPE THE MULLIONS AND DECORATE THE DOOR:** Tint ¼ cup icing with a few drops of violet food coloring. Scrape into a pastry bag fitted with the #2 plain tip and pipe the mullions, 1 vertical line and 1 horizontal line on each window, except for the arched window above the door and

the door itself; edge these in violet with piped violet panels. Glue the silver dragées in place as doorknobs.

9. **PIPE THE WINDOW AND DOOR TRIM:** Color I cup white icing deep pink and scrape into a pastry bag fitted with the #47 basket-weave tip and use the plain side to pipe around each window and the doorway. Let stand to dry for about I hour.

10. **ASSEMBLE THE HOUSE:** If you are illuminating your house, see page 13. Color about I cup icing brown, if you like, or use plain white icing. Fit a pastry bag with the #7 plain tip and fill with the icing. Pipe icing along the bottom edge of the front of the house. Position it where you want it to stand on the board, leaving room for the entryway, and place a heavy mug or can on each side to help it stand upright until the icing dries. Pipe icing along the bottom edge and front edge of I of the side pieces and attach the side to the front so the side edge of the side is flush against the back of the front piece. Repeat with the remaining side piece and the rear facade piece, adding more mugs for support as necessary. Insert straight

pins through the front wall into each side wall and through the back wall into each side wall. Pipe icing along the bottom and one side of each interior support piece. Glue 2 supports to the base and in between the windows of the back wall. Glue the last 2 supports to the base and in between the windows on the front wall. Secure with straight pins.

11. Pipe icing around the top edges of the house. Rest the roof support piece (A) on the edges. Let stand to dry for about I hour.

12. Pipe icing along the side edges of the front entry piece. Ice one side edge of the front entry side piece and attach to the front entry piece. Repeat with the second front entry side piece. Pipe icing along the side edges of the entry and attach to the front facade. Pipe icing around the top edges and rest piece G on the edges. Let stand to dry for about I hour. Wrap the tip of the pastry bag with plastic wrap and refrigerate until you are ready to continue. Let stand until the icing is dry, about I hour. Remove the pins.

13. **ATTACH THE ROOF:** Pipe icing on the bottom and side edges of roof

more second empire style

The French use the term *horror vacui*—figuratively, the fear of unembellished surfaces—to describe the highly ornamented Second Empire style, so have no fear of overdoing it when it comes to decoration. If you'd like to add to the ornamentation we've already suggested, here are some suggestions:

- Dormer windows that project like eyebrows from the roof.
- Bay windows and/or balconies supported by brackets.
- A cupola (a small dome) set atop the roof.

pieces B, C, D, and E. Arrange them on top of the roof support and leaning against each other. Secure with straight pins. Repeat with the entry roof pieces H, I, J, and K. Let stand until the icing is dry, about I hour. Using the pastry bag fitted with the #45 plain tip, pipe deep pink icing along the top edges of the house and two-story entry roof pieces and set the flat roof pieces F and L on top of each section. Use the deep pink icing to glue the pacifier candy brackets underneath the roof overhang, evenly spacing them. Color some icing ivory and scrape into a

pastry bag fitted with the #47 basket-weave tip. Use the grooved side to pipe trim all the way around the roof right at the edge of the overhang.

14. PIPE AND ATTACH THE FRET-WORK: Place a sheet of parchment paper over the fretwork templates and use a pastry bag fitted with the #3 plain tip and filled with white icing to pipe the metal fretwork onto the paper. The gingerbread will often change size when baked, so double-check the length of the rooftops and adjust the template if necessary. Spread a layer of white icing on the top of the roof.

15. TRIM THE ROOF: Using white icing and a pastry bag fitted with the #47 basket-weave tip, pipe white icing along the top edge of the rooftops. Let the piping dry completely. Mix the gold luster dust with the alcohol. Using sweeping strokes and a flat-edge brush, apply gold paint to the rooftop, the piped roof, and the piped trim on the lower eave. Let dry for about 1 hour and then use white icing to glue

the fretwork to the top of the main roof and the entry roof.

16. ASSEMBLE THE STAIRS AND THE PORTICO ROOF: Using icing, glue the gingerbread stair tread supports to the base of the portico and then glue the individual treads in place. Glue the landing into place on top of the stairs. Working with the portico flat support roof and the candy sticks at the same time, use brown icing to glue the sticks to the landing floor and rest the roof on top of them. Glue the portico architrave to the roof. Glue the portico sloped roof pieces in place with the top peak running front to back. Glue a piece of log-shaped Bazooka bubble gum at the base of the staircase on each side. Glue a gum ball to the top of each piece of log-shaped gum. Let stand to dry for about 1 hour.

17. MAKE AND ATTACH THE HIGH FOUNDATION BASE: Trim any overlapping corners of the foundation base with a handheld grater or a rasp. Glue each piece of the gingerbread base to the bottom

20. SHINGLE THE ROOF: Cut the Sour Power Belts into 1-inch pieces and then use the large end of a pastry bag tip to cut away 1 end of each piece for a rounded edge. Squeeze a little bit of icing on the Power Belt pieces, one at a time, and apply a row of pieces along the bottom edge of one side of the roof. Apply another row above this one, slightly overlapping it. Continue until you reach the peak of the roof, making about 9 rows on the main roof and 10 on the entry portico roof.

21. MAKE THE CHIMNEYS AND FLUES: Reserve 4 caramels and cut the remaining 16 caramels in half. Use white icing to glue them together, stacking them, to make 2 chimneys on one side of the roof. Heat the remaining 4 caramels in the microwave for 2 to 5 seconds, just to soften them. Stretch each so it is long enough to make a smooth edge on top of each chimney and glue it to a chimney with white icing. Cut the Twizzler into 4 pieces and glue 2 pieces onto each chimney.

22. LANDSCAPE THE HOUSE: Combine the coconut and a few drops of bright green food coloring in the work bowl of a food processor and pulse several times until the coconut is green. Tint 1 cup (or more if necessary) icing with bright green food coloring and spread in a thin layer over the board surrounding the house. Press the green coconut into the icing.

23. Use an electric drill with a small drill bit to drill holes through the watermelon gum balls (alternatively, use a hammer and a nail). Push 2 gum balls onto each pretzel stick so that about $1/2$ inch of pretzel stick is exposed at one end. Push that end into the top of a Rolo candy. Glue the topiaries to the grass on each side of the entry.

of the house with icing. Cut the Airhead Extremes similarly and attach to the house above the foundation base with icing.

18. PIPE THE UPPER TRIM BOARD AND ENTRY TRIM BOARDS: Fill a pastry bag fitted with the #47 basket-weave tip with ivory icing and pipe a trim board near the roof and all the way around the house. Pipe a trim board on each side of the front door, right at the edges of the entry.

19. PIPE THE CORNERSTONES: Use the ivory icing and the #47 basket-weave tip to pipe cornerstones, alternating short and long ones, at each corner of the house from bottom to top.

ADIRONDACK CAMP

SEE TEMPLATES ON PAGE 117

Our gingerbread version of the late-nineteenth-century RUSTIC vacation retreat is modest in scale, with these distinctive features: a SIMPLE RECTANGULAR FORM with overhang roofs, decorative WOOD TWIG (pretzel) trim, a STONE CHIMNEY and a ROCK FOUNDATION made of chocolate candy rocks and icing mortar, horizontally and vertically laid WOOD LOGS (etched gingerbread) forming exterior walls, and roof SHINGLES made of gum sticks. Dashes of color, often red or blue, are common in Adirondack camps, so the door of our house is piped with blue icing. A bluebird sculpted from fondant or a pair of skis cut out from red chewing gum would add some color and whimsy.

INGREDIENTS

1½ RECIPES GINGER-BREAD DOUGH (PAGE 83), CHILLED

1 16-OUNCE BAG BUTTERSCOTCH CANDIES, CRUSHED IN A FOOD PROCESSOR

1 RECIPE ROYAL ICING (PAGE 84)

BROWN, BLUE, AND GREEN FOOD COLORING

1 SMALL BLACK LICORICE NIB

1 ICE CREAM SUGAR CONE

1 TEASPOON SMALL COLORED DRAGÉES

1½ CUPS CANDY ROCKS (ABOUT 1 POUND)

1 2.7-OUNCE PACKAGE POCKY-BRAND HAZELNUT AND MILK CHOCOLATE–COVERED PRETZELS OR PLAIN POCKY STICKS

10 2¼-OUNCE PACKS BIG RED GUM

1 LARGE TOOTSIE ROLL

½ CUP DARK BROWN J ELLY BEANS (ABOUT 3 OUNCES)

1 SMALL TOOTSIE ROLL

1 SMALL PIECE RED FRUIT LEATHER (FROM 1½-OUNCE PACKAGE)

special equipment

16 X 20-INCH CUTTING BOARD OR FOIL-COVERED STYROFOAM BOARD

PASTRY BAGS AND #2 PLAIN TIP, #47 BASKET-WEAVE TIP, #67 LEAF TIP, AND #7 PLAIN TIP

CAKE COMB

CONSTRUCTION NOTE

The gingerbread chimney may look rather small, but when covered with candy rocks it becomes massive. Compare the rocks you've bought with the ones in the photo. If yours are quite a bit larger, you may want to make your chimney even smaller to compensate.

HISTORICAL NOTE

This style is associated with the great camps of the Adirondack Mountains of New York, built in the second half of the nineteenth century by wealthy vacationers who wanted to live in rustic luxury. The houses, influenced by both Swiss chalets and traditional Japanese architecture, were constructed of native building materials for the aesthetic purpose of harmonizing with nature but also to save on the expense of transporting materials to such a remote location. Whole, split, and peeled logs and granite fieldstone were used in interiors as well as exteriors. Massive fireplaces and chimneys made of cut stone were also common elements. Roof overhangs prevented ice and snow from building up against walls. The houses were raised off the ground and built on rock foundations to prevent dampness.

more adirondack style

You might consider adding these decorations, which mimic the rustic materials used in Adirondack camps:

- Tree limbs and roots. With natural curves and knots, these were often used to create ornamental patterns on the outside of the houses. To imitate this effect, you could use Tootsie Rolls, briefly softened in the microwave if necessary, to make more elaborate porch railings and even furniture to decorate the porch.

- Fish and game trophies, commonly used to decorate the interior of Adirondack houses. A small Swedish fish, mounted on a gingerbread plaque and hung over the door, could allude to this custom.

1. BAKE THE GINGERBREAD: Enlarge the templates on pieces of thin cardboard or sturdy paper and cut to size. Preheat the oven to 375°F.

2. Divide the dough into 5 equal pieces. Wrap 4 pieces tightly in plastic wrap and keep in the refrigerator. Lightly flour a piece of parchment paper and roll out the fifth piece of dough onto the parchment so it is ¼ inch thick. Place the template for the front of the house on the dough and cut around the template with a sharp knife. Cut away the door opening and set aside the door piece. Cut away the windows. Use a ruler to score the front of the house with deep horizontal lines about ½ inch apart. Remove the scraps from the parchment, wrap them in plastic, and refrigerate.

3. Slide the parchment onto a rimless baking sheet. Place the door piece next to the front piece on the baking sheet, at least 1 inch away from it. Slide the baking sheet into the

oven and bake until the door is firm, about 10 minutes. Use a metal spatula to remove the door to a wire rack to cool. Continue to bake the house until the edges are lightly browned and the center is firm, 2 to 4 minutes more. Let the front piece cool on the baking sheet for 5 minutes. Sprinkle crushed butterscotch candy into each window space, completely filling it with a thin layer, and return the baking sheet to the oven until the candy is melted, 5 to 7 minutes. Remove the pan from the oven again and let the gingerbread cool completely before sliding the piece, still on the parchment, off of the pan.

4. Working in 3 batches and using 3 of the remaining pieces of dough plus scraps, repeat the rolling and baking with the back and 2 side pieces, adding the window glass as before and baking again until melted. Score the back and sides of the house.

5. Roll out the remaining piece of dough and cut out all roof pieces, the porch deck, porch supports, front step, and chimney pieces. Bake in one final batch until the edges are lightly browned and the center is firm, 12 to 14 minutes. Slide the pieces, still on the parchment, onto wire racks to cool completely.

6. When the pieces are cool, transfer them to baking sheets and tightly cover the sheets in plastic until you are ready to assemble the house. They will keep for up to 1 week.

7. PIPE BETWEEN THE LOGS: Fit a pastry bag with the #2 plain tip and fill with icing. Pipe thin lines along the score marks on the front, back, and sides of the house. Wrap the tip of the pastry bag with plastic wrap and refrigerate until needed. Let the house stand to dry for about 1 hour.

8. PIPE THE WINDOW TRIM: Place ½ cup icing in a small bowl and use food coloring to tint it a dark brown. Scrape the icing into a pastry bag fitted with the #47 basket-weave tip and pipe around each window. Switch to the #2 plain tip and pipe the mullions, one horizontal and one vertical, onto each window. Cover the tip of the pastry bag with plastic wrap and refrigerate. Let the house stand to dry for about 1 hour.

9. COLOR THE DOOR AND ATTACH THE HARDWARE: Fill a small bowl with 3 tablespoons icing and tint it with a few drops of blue food coloring to make it bright blue. Smooth the colored icing over the door and use a cake comb to score it to look like wood grain. Cut 2 small triangles and a small round from the licorice nib and attach as hinges and knob. Set aside to allow the icing to harden completely, about 2 hours.

10. MAKE THE CHRISTMAS TREE: Tint ¼ cup icing with a few drops of green food coloring. Scrape into a pastry bag fitted with the #67 leaf tip and pipe greenery, working around the ice cream cone from the wide end to the tip. Use tweezers to dot the tree with dragées. Let stand to dry for about 2 hours.

11. ASSEMBLE THE HOUSE: If you are illuminating your house, see page 13. Color about 1 cup icing brown, if you like, or use plain white icing. Fit a pastry bag with the #7 plain tip and fill with the icing. Keep the rest of the icing in a bowl, pressing a piece of plastic wrap against the surface to prevent it from drying out. Pipe icing along the bottom edge of the front piece A. Position it where you want it to stand on the board, leaving ample room in front for the porch, and place a heavy mug or can on each side to help it stand upright until the icing dries. Pipe icing along the bottom edge and front edge of piece B and attach it to the right side of piece A so the side edge of the side is flush against the back of the front piece. Repeat with piece C, attaching it to the left side, and then attach rear piece D. adding more mugs for support as necessary. Insert straight pins through the front wall into each side wall and through the back wall into each side wall. Wrap the tip of the pastry bag with plastic wrap and refrigerate until you are ready to continue. Let stand until the icing is dry, about 1 hour. Remove the mugs and pins.

12. PIPE THE CORNER BOARDS: Using the pastry bag fitted with the #47 basket-weave tip and filled with brown icing, pipe the corner boards at each corner of the house. Let stand to dry for about 1 hour.

13. ASSEMBLE THE CHIMNEY: Pipe icing along the sides of the pieces to glue them to each other. Let stand to dry for 15 minutes.

14. COVER THE CHIMNEY WITH ROCKS AND LAY THE PORCH FOUNDATION: Spread a thin layer of icing over the chimney and attach the candy rocks. Let stand to dry for at least 1 hour. Pipe icing along one long edge of the porch rear support piece. Glue to the center of the front of the house. Pipe icing along one long edge of the 2 porch side supports, and glue at either end of the rear support piece so that the rear is flush with the sides. Pipe icing along the exposed short edges of the side supports and one long edge of the front support piece. Glue the front support piece flush to the side supports. Spread a thin layer of icing over the exposed sides and the top edge of the porch supports, pipe icing onto the long cabin edge of the porch deck, and place the deck on the supports. Attach the candy rocks to the 3 exposed faces of the icing-covered porch supports.

15. Glue the rock-covered chimney to the side of the house.

16. ATTACH THE DOOR: Glue the door to the doorway with icing.

17. **ATTACH THE ROOF:** Double-check that the roof pieces fit around the chimney, filing them with a handheld grater or a rasp if necessary. Pipe icing along each side edge of 1 roof piece. Position the roof piece on top of the house, lining it up so its top edge runs from point to point of the sides of the house. Secure the roof piece by inserting a straight pin through the front and back of the house and into the roof at the peak and at the eaves. Repeat with the second roof piece. Let stand until the icing is dry, about 1 hour. Remove the pins.

18. **ATTACH THE PORCH ROOF AND ROOF SUPPORTS:** Pipe icing along the front edge of the main roof and at both ends of 4 Pocky Sticks. Glue the Pocky Stick supports to the porch deck. Position the porch roof to rest on top of the Pocky Sticks while attaching it to the house roof. An extra pair of hands is very helpful for this procedure. Let stand to dry for about 1 hour.

19. **SHINGLE THE ROOF:** Meanwhile, cut the gum pieces into thirds. Save 2 pieces of gum

for skis. Squeeze a little bit of icing on the gum pieces, one at a time, and apply a row of gum pieces along the bottom edge of one side of the roof. Apply another row above this one, slightly overlapping it. Continue until you reach the peak of the roof, making about 12 rows in total. Repeat with the other side of the roof.

20. **MAKE THE PORCH RAILINGS:** Color ¼ cup icing brown and scrape it into a pastry bag fitted with the #2 plain tip. Pipe icing into both ends of 2 Pocky Sticks and position at the front of the porch deck and under the porch roof to frame the porch entry. Use additional Pocky Sticks, breaking them as necessary, to make the porch railings; glue them together with brown icing. Briefly heat the large Tootsie Roll in a microwave (5 to 10 seconds should do it) or roll between the palms of your hands to soften it, and then cut and roll it into twig-like branches and attach to the railings.

21. **MAKE THE FRONT PORCH STEP:** Glue the porch step to the board in front of the porch. Glue a row of candy rocks to the board in front of the porch the same length and width as the front step. Glue the step to the rocks.

22. **LANDSCAPE THE HOUSE:** Use a small spatula to spread icing over the exposed board. Arrange the jelly beans in a cobblestone pattern in front of the step. Glue the tree to the snow. With icing, build fences out of the remaining Pocky Sticks, reserving 1. Mold the small softened Tootsie Roll into a mailbox shape. Cut a small flag from fruit leather and attach it to the mailbox with icing. Push into the remaining Pocky Stick to create the mailbox. Push the other end of the Pocky Stick into a small piece of the remaining large Tootsie Roll to create a stable base. Glue the mailbox on the base, set it in front of the fence, and cover the base of the mailbox with white icing to resemble snow.

URBAN BROWNSTONE

SEE TEMPLATES ON PAGE 121

Our gingerbread brownstone has features that will be familiar to anyone who has walked a brownstone-lined block: STEPS AND STOOP leading to a second-floor entrance, an OFF-CENTER FRONT DOOR, HEAVY CORNICES (the horizontal trim) on the upper part of the building, and RUSTICATION (the boldly textured surface of rough-hewn blocks) on the lower half.

special equipment

3 PIECES 12 x 18-INCH CORRUGATED CARD-BOARD, EACH 1/4 INCH OR 3/8 INCH THICK

FONDANT ROLLER, OPTIONAL

PASTRY BAGS AND #2 PLAIN TIP AND #7 PLAIN TIP

2 12-INCH PIECES OF SATIN RIBBON

NONSTICK VEGETABLE OIL SPRAY

POINTSETTIA MOLDS, OPTIONAL

INGREDIENTS

2 RECIPES GINGER-BREAD DOUGH (PAGE 83), CHILLED

1 16-OUNCE BAG BUTTERSCOTCH CANDIES, CRUSHED IN A FOOD PROCESSOR

1 1/2 RECIPES ROYAL ICING (PAGE 84)

VIOLET, RED, ORANGE, IVORY, BROWN, AND GREEN FOOD COLORING

2 RECIPES PASTILLAGE (PAGE 85)

CONFECTIONERS' SUGAR

1 1/2 POUNDS FONDANT (SEE RESOURCES, PAGE 86)

ABOUT 16 ROUND PURPLE SPREE CANDIES (FROM ABOUT 5 1.77-OUNCE ROLLS)

2 1/2-OUNCE PACKAGES DARK RASPBERRY FRUIT LEATHER

ABOUT 30 CONCORD CANDY BLOX (ABOUT 1 OUNCE)

2 YELLOW BANANA LAFFY TAFFY CHUNKS

2 RED LICORICE NIBS

2 GOLD DRAGÉES

4 SMALL TOOTSIE ROLLS

2 SMALL MALTED MILK BALLS

3 1/2-OUNCE PACKAGES TINY CHICLETS

1 RECIPE GREEN RICE KRISPIE TREATS (PAGE 44)

1 TABLESPOON COLORED DRAGÉES

2 ROLOS (CHOCOLATE-AND-CARAMEL CANDIES)

1/2 CUP RED SANDING SUGAR

HISTORICAL NOTE

Row houses sheathed in brown sandstone were built in Northeastern cities beginning in the mid-1800s. A popular form of upper-middle-class housing, they featured imposing staircases, heavy cornices, and stone architraves and windowsills as well as elaborate Victorian interior décor. Like today's suburban subdivisions, brownstones were often built block by block on undeveloped land. They dominated upper-middle-class development in New York City, Philadelphia, and Boston—and later in Chicago—until the automobile made longer commutes practical and housing development shifted to the suburbs.

CONSTRUCTION NOTES

It took us a while to figure out how best to re-create in sugar the rustication, cornice, and window trim that characterize the brownstone. After trying different combinations of icing and candy, we settled on rolled fondant for the rustication and pastillage for the cornice and window trim. We loved the way the fondant smoothly covered the gingerbread. Rather than coloring it brown, which would have made the building too drab for our taste, we colored the fondant ivory. The result is so elegant! The pastillage gave us the crisp, sharp edges we wanted for the trim. As we were mixing a batch anyway, we decided to make the door from the pastillage, too. Alternatively, you could spread Royal Icing over the bottom half of the house to stand in for rustication, cut the door and the cornice out of gingerbread, and use Trident or Dentyne chewing gum (which is just the right size) for the window trim.

Because the roof is not covered in shingles the way so many of our other roofs are, we thought it would be fun to be able to remove it in case a window needed to be repaired from within. Gingerbread supports glued to the inside walls of the house support the recessed roof. Put the roof in place by sliding pieces of wide ribbon underneath it and lowering it onto the supports, letting some of the ribbon peek out. Lift the roof off by grasping the exposed ribbon and carefully pulling up.

PROCEDURE

1. **BAKE THE GINGERBREAD:** Enlarge the templates on pieces of thin cardboard or sturdy paper and cut to size. Preheat the oven to 375°F.

2. Divide the dough into 5 equal pieces. Wrap 4 pieces tightly in plastic wrap and keep in the refrigerator. Lightly flour a piece of parchment paper and roll out the fifth piece of the dough onto the parchment so it is ¼ inch thick. Place the template for the front of the house on the dough and cut around the template with a sharp knife. Cut away the door opening. Cut away the windows. Remove the scraps from the parchment, wrap them in plastic, and refrigerate until ready to reroll.

3. Slide the parchment onto a rimless baking sheet. Slide the baking sheet into the oven and bake until the edges are lightly browned and the center is firm, 12 to 14 minutes. Remove from the oven and let cool on the pan for 5 minutes.

4. Sprinkle crushed butterscotch candy into the window spaces, filling the spaces completely with a thin layer, and return the baking sheet to the oven until the candy is melted, 5 to 7 minutes. Remove the pan from the oven again and let the gingerbread cool completely before sliding the gingerbread, still on the parchment, off the pan and continuing.

5. Working in 3 batches and using 3 of the remaining pieces of dough plus scraps, repeat the rolling and baking with the back and 2 side pieces, adding window glass as before and baking again until melted.

6. Roll out the remaining piece of dough along with the scraps and cut the roof and support pieces, stair pieces, and the cornice pieces and door if making them out of gingerbread. Bake in one batch until the edges are lightly browned and the center is firm, 7 to 8 minutes for the small pieces, 12 to 14 minutes for the large ones. Slide the pieces, still on the parchment, onto wire racks to cool completely.

7. When the pieces are cool, transfer them to baking sheets and tightly cover the sheets in plastic until you are ready to assemble the house. They will keep for up to 1 week.

more urban brownstone style

Take a walk down a brownstone-lined street to gather more decorating ideas for your house. Here are a few that we like:

- Add a door at the garden level: A door on the inside staircase wall, leading to a lower interior level, would be an authentic touch.

- Make a street lamp by using a striped candy-cane stick for a lamppost with a yellow gumdrop for the lantern. Turn the gumdrop upside down, and with dark brown icing, glue the narrow top to the candy-cane base. Pipe the top and sides of the lantern with the brown icing and pipe green holly with red berries around the base of the lantern and the bottom of the candy-cane post. Glue the post to the gingerbread house base.

8. PIPE THE MULLIONS: Spoon ¼ cup icing into a small bowl and tint with a few drops of violet food coloring. Scrape into a pastry bag fitted with the #2 plain tip and pipe the mullions—I vertical line and 3 horizontal lines—onto the candy windows on the front and rear pieces. Pipe I horizontal and I vertical line onto the candy windows on the side pieces. Set the pieces aside to dry for about I hour.

9. ROLL AND CUT THE WINDOW ARCHITRAVE PIECES: Knead a few drops of red food coloring into ⅓ cup pastillage. Lightly flour a countertop with confectioners' sugar and roll out the pastillage to a ⅛-inch thickness. Cut 12 rectangles, each measuring 1⅝ inches across and ¼ inch high. Cut 12 smaller pieces, each measuring 1⅞ inches across and ⅛ inch high. Set aside to dry overnight.

10. ROLL AND CUT THE DOOR: Cut pieces B out of thick cardboard. Glue pieces B onto piece A to look like panels on a door. Repeat the process with the rear and cellar door

templates. Tint another piece of pastillage with a few drops or more of orange food coloring to achieve a bright orange. Roll out to a ¼-inch thickness. Spray the door template with nonstick vegetable oil spray. Set the template, cardboard panel–side down, on top of the pastillage and press on the template lightly to make the panel impressions. Use a sharp paring knife to cut around the template. Remove the template. Set aside the door to dry overnight. Repeat this process with the rear and cellar door templates, if using.

11. ROLL AND CUT THE CORNICE: Tint ½ cup pastillage with a few drops or more of violet to make it deep purple. Roll out to a 9 x 2-inch rectangle, ¼ inch thick. Use the cornice templates as a guide and use a sharp paring knife to cut the 2 cornice pieces ⅜ inch in thickness. Stand a ruler about ¼ inch from the bottom of the thinner bottom cornice piece and use one of the purple Spree candies to make a rounded impression in the piece every ¼ inch. Set aside the cornice pieces to dry overnight. Save the leftover violet pastillage for window boxes.

12. ROLL OUT, CUT, AND ATTACH THE FONDANT FOR RUSTICATION: Cut small pieces of parchment to protect the candy windows on the bottom half of the front facade. Lay a piece of parchment on top of each window. Lightly dust a countertop with confectioners' sugar. Set aside ¼ cup of fondant, covered. Tint the rest ivory with a few drops of ivory food coloring. Roll the ivory fondant into a 10 x 9-inch rectangle about ⅛ inch thick. Run a fondant roller fitted with the straight line cutter lightly across the rectangle, making horizontal impressions in the fondant but not cutting through it. Alternatively, you can lightly score it with the dull edge of a paring knife at 1-inch intervals.

Use the knife to trim it so it will fit over the bottom half of the front facade. Spread a thin layer of icing over the bottom half of the front facade and lay the fondant on top of it. Gently press the fondant into the window openings and cut the fondant that is over the openings. Lift away the extra fondant with tweezers and remove the parchment paper. Let the icing under the fondant dry for 1 hour. An over-the-door pediment and door side pilasters are included in the template as an optional door treatment.

13. ASSEMBLE THE HOUSE: If you are illuminating your house, see page 13. Color about 1 cup icing brown, if you like, or use plain white icing. Fit a pastry bag with the #7 plain tip and fill with the icing. Keep the rest of the icing in a bowl, pressing a piece of plastic wrap against the surface to prevent it from drying out. Pipe icing along the bottom edge of the front piece of the house. Position it where you want it to stand on the board and place a heavy mug or can on each side to help it stand upright until the icing dries. Pipe

icing along the bottom edge and front edge of a side piece and attach to the front so that the longer side edge of the side piece is flush against the back of the front piece. Repeat with the other side and the back, adding more mugs for support as necessary. Insert straight pins through the front wall into each side wall and through the back wall into each side wall. Wrap the tip of the pastry bag with plastic wrap and refrigerate until ready to continue. Let stand until the icing is dry, about 1 hour. Remove the mugs and pins.

14. ATTACH THE ROOF SUPPORTS: With icing, glue the 2 side roof supports perpendicularly to the inside of each side piece, and the 2 front supports to the inside of the front facade, between the windows and reaching about 1 inch from the top edges of the sides. Place the 2 center back supports inside the building and glue the inside of the

base and the rear wall, between the windows, with icing.

15. CONSTRUCT THE STAIRS: With icing, glue the gingerbread stair stringer supports to the inside of each staircase wall, making sure that the supports line up. Grate the stair treads and landing platform with a handheld grater or a rasp if necessary to make them smooth and even, and glue the stair treads and landing to the stair supports, connecting the walls with the treads. Let stand to dry for 15 minutes. Cut the fruit leather into long thin rectangles the same size as the empty spaces between the stair treads and press them into the spaces, using icing if necessary (the fruit leather is sticky, and you will probably be able to press it into place without icing). Glue the staircase to the front of the house with icing.

16. MAKE THE CHIMNEY: Snap together the Candy Blox to make the chimney, about 5 bricks tall. Stretch and trim the Laffy Taffy Chunks and glue them around the top edge of the chimney. Glue the licorice nibs to the top of the chimney. Set aside.

17. ATTACH THE ARCHITRAVES AND FRONT DOOR: Use icing to glue a small architrave piece over each of the 6 upper windows on the front facade, the 6 upper windows of the rear facade, and the window on each side. Glue a larger architrave piece over each of the smaller pieces above the 6 upper windows on the front facade (the side and rear windows don't have this second architrave piece). Glue 2 gold dragées to the door for doorknobs. Glue the door to the front facade.

18. ATTACH THE CORNICE: Use icing to glue a purple Spree candy into each of the bottom cornice piece impressions. Let stand to dry for about 15 minutes. Glue the bottom

cornice piece to the upper ¾ inch of the front facade. Glue the upper cornice piece to the top edge of the facade, inserting straight pins through the side of the cornice and into the front facade. Let stand to dry for about 1 hour.

19. MAKE THE STAIRCASE POSTS: Microwave a Tootsie Roll for 2 to 4 seconds to soften it. Mold the Tootsie Roll into a ¾-inch square shape and glue it to the foot of one of the staircase walls. Repeat with another Tootsie Roll, gluing it to the other foot of the staircase. Microwave a third Tootsie Roll and roll it into a tube shape about 1½ inches tall. Use icing to glue it to a square Tootsie Roll. Repeat with the remaining Tootsie Roll. Glue a malted milk ball on top of each Tootsie Roll tube.

20. LANDSCAPE THE HOUSE: Spread a thin layer of icing over the recessed portion of the exposed board. Arrange the Chiclets in a checkerboard pattern with a pair of tweezers. Pipe brown icing onto the underside of the single stair tread and place

it at the center front edge of the Chiclet-covered recess.

21. MAKE THE WINDOW BOXES: Take the remaining violet pastillage and using 2 rulers, shape the pastillage into a long thin rectangle with a square section. Measure the width of each window on the front facade. Cut the long piece of pastillage into sections to fit in the windowsills.

22. MAKE THE FONDANT SIDEWALK: For the front sidewalk, roll out the reserved white fondant, cut a straight edge, and roll over a rolling pin. Smooth a layer of icing over the sidewalk area and gently unroll the fondant over it, aligning the straight edge of the fondant with the edge of the front steps and recessed area. Trim extra fondant with a sharp knife. Create a brick pattern in the fondant by pressing the edge of a ruler into the fondant for the long lines and using a knife to make the shorter lines. Let the fondant dry in place.

23. MAKE THE RICE KRISPIE SHRUBS AND WREATH: Divide the green-tinted Rice Krispie mixture into 3 portions. Form 2 of the portions into 2 separate hedges that line both sides of the house. Form the remaining portion into a large wreath and decorate the wreath with dragées. Tint ¾ cup icing with 5 drops green food coloring and pipe green-tinted icing onto the side of the building in the shape of the wreath and attach the wreath. Smooth green-tinted icing on the exposed surface of the board and glue the hedges in place.

24. MAKE THE POINSETTIAS: Knead red food coloring into 3 tablespoons pastillage. If the pastillage is too sticky, knead in a little confectioners' sugar. We used a store-bought mold for our poinsettia flowers but you can always create your own flowers and leaves. Spray the mold with nonstick vegetable oil spray and press the red pastillage into the mold; remove and let dry. Tint 3 tablespoons of pastillage green with 2 or 3 drops of food coloring and repeat with green-tinted pastillage for the poinsettia leaves. Let the flowers and leaves dry overnight. Place a dab of icing onto the Rolo candies and glue poinsettia leaves and flowers onto the Rolos. Place 1 Rolo in front of the cellar door and 1 at the top of the stairs. Pipe icing onto the backs of the remaining poinsettia flowers and leaves and place on various window boxes of the brownstone.

25. COAT THE ROOF WITH SUGAR: Place the sanding sugar in a pan and gently shake to level. Ice the surface of the roof with red-tinted icing and place the roof, icing side down, into the red sugar. Remove the roof. Sprinkle the remaining red sugar over any bald spots on the roof surface, shake off excess sugar back into the pan, and set aside to dry for 1 hour.

26. SET IN THE ROOF AND POSITION THE CHIMNEY: Slide the 2 pieces of ribbon under the roof. Drop the sugared roof into the house so that it rests on the supports, leaving a little bit of ribbon peeking out of each side. Position the chimney on one side of the roof, but don't glue it on, so you can remove it before removing the roof piece. To lift the roof off the house, carefully pull up the pieces of ribbon.

TUDOR REVIVAL

SEE TEMPLATES ON PAGE 127

INGREDIENTS

- 1½ RECIPES GINGERBREAD DOUGH (PAGE 83), CHILLED

- 6 PIECES CLEAR SHEET GELATIN WITH CROSS-HATCHING

- 2 RECIPES ROYAL ICING (PAGE 84)

- ORANGE, PINK, GREEN, BLUE, AND YELLOW FOOD COLORING

- 1 BLACK LICORICE LACE

- ABOUT 24 BLACK TWIZZLERS (FROM 1 16-OUNCE BAG)

- 2 SILVER DRAGÉES

- ABOUT 30 LARGE MARSHMALLOWS (FROM 1 10-OUNCE BAG)

- 1 TABLESPOON GREEN SANDING SUGAR

- 2 1-POUND BAGS BASSETT'S LICORICE ALLSORTS

- 1 18-OUNCE BOX SPOON-SIZE SHREDDED WHEAT 'N BRAN

- 3 STRIPED CANDY STICKS

Our Tudor Revival has a STEEPLY PITCHED ROOF, a cantilevered jetty overhanging the entry door, prominent cross gables, small DIAMOND-SHAPED WINDOWPANES, a vertical planked door, and, of course, the decorative HALF-TIMBERING that characterizes the style. Taking our cue from the black licorice timbers, we have decorated the house economically by using the colorful candies in two bags of licorice allsorts to make the walkway and front entry pillars, roof pinnacles, trim boards, and wreath. Instead of shingles, we've chosen spoon-size shredded wheat that resembles false THATCHED ROOFING, more popular in England than in the United States but irresistible in a gingerbread house nonetheless. A low hedge made of marshmallows covered with green icing completes the landscape.

CONSTRUCTION NOTES

It's important to take your time and build this house in stages because the stability of the cantilevered jetty overhang depends on all of its parts being glued firmly to the main house (the gingerbread brackets are purely decorative and do not support the weight of the overhang). Attach the side walls first, using icing and straight pins, and let the icing dry completely. Then attach the facade, again using straight pins as well as icing, and let dry. Finally, put the roof on and let dry again before proceeding with the decoration of the house. Always remember to remove the pins!

special equipment

16 x 20-INCH CUTTING BOARD OR FOIL-COVERED STYROFOAM BOARD

PASTRY BAGS AND #2 PLAIN TIP, #7 PLAIN TIP, AND #47 BASKET-WEAVE TIP

Tudor Revival houses, very loosely based on medieval buildings (not, as the name suggests, on English buildings from the sixteenth century), became popular in American suburbs in the 1920s. They were built in many shapes and sizes, from humble cottages to grand mansions. But all displayed the false half-timbering (the heavy beams filled in with masonry serve a decorative rather than structural purpose) meant to suggest construction techniques from an earlier time.

1. **BAKE THE GINGERBREAD:** Enlarge the templates on pieces of thin cardboard or sturdy paper and cut to size. Preheat the oven to 375°F.

2. Divide the dough into 7 equal pieces. Wrap 6 pieces tightly in plastic wrap and keep in the refrigerator. Lightly flour a piece of parchment paper and roll out the seventh piece of dough so it is ¼ inch thick. Place the template for the front of the house on the dough and cut around the template with a sharp knife. Cut away the door opening and set aside the door piece. Cut away the windows. Remove the scraps from the parchment, wrap them in plastic, and refrigerate.

3. Slide the parchment onto a rimless baking sheet. Place the door piece next to the front piece on the baking sheet, at least 1 inch away from it. Slide the baking sheet into the oven and bake until the door is firm, about 10 minutes. Use a metal spatula to remove the door to a wire rack to cool. Continue to bake the house until the edges are lightly browned and the center is firm, 2 to 4 minutes more. Slide the parchment onto a wire rack and let cool completely.

4. Working in 6 batches and using the 6 remaining pieces of dough plus scraps, repeat the rolling and baking with the back, 2 sides, all roof pieces, overhang pieces, and chimney pieces. (Score the chimney to look like bricks.)

5. When the pieces are cool, transfer them to baking sheets and tightly cover the sheets in plastic until you are ready to assemble the house. They will keep for up to 1 week.

6. **ATTACH THE WINDOWS AND PIPE THE WINDOWPANES:** Cut the sheet gelatin into pieces slightly larger than each

---

more tudor revival style

Quirky Tudor Revivals mixed and matched many design elements in an almost infinite number of ways. Any of the following would add an authentic touch to your gingerbread Tudor:

- Brick wall cladding, in elaborate patterns if you like.
- Stone wall cladding.
- A side porch, also with small-paned windows.

---

of the windows. Spoon ¼ cup icing into a small bowl and tint with 1 drop of orange food coloring. Scrape into a pastry bag fitted with the #2 plain tip. Lay the front and side pieces facedown on a work surface, and glue the gelatin pieces to the windows. Let dry for 15 minutes and then flip the pieces over. Following the cross-hatching, pipe diagonal lines over each of the windows to create windowpanes. Let dry for 15 minutes.

7. **COLOR THE DOORS AND ATTACH THE HARDWARE:** Spoon ¼ cup icing into a small bowl and tint with a drop of pink food coloring. Use a small offset spatula to ice the front and back door pieces. Cut lengths of the black licorice lace and press them into the doors vertically to create door panels. Cut 4 triangles from a Twizzler and place 2 on each door as hinges. Press a dragée doorknob into each door. Let dry for 2 hours.

8. **COLOR THE SHRUBBERY:** Spoon ⅔ cup icing in a medium bowl and tint with 1 or 2 drops of green food coloring. Line a baking sheet with parchment paper. Smooth the icing all over the sides and top of each marshmallow with a small metal spatula, pulling the spatula away from the icing to

create little peaks. Set the marshmallows, uniced-side down, on the parchment and sprinkle with the sanding sugar. Let stand to dry for about 1 hour.

9. **ASSEMBLE THE HOUSE:** If you are illuminating your house, see page 13. Fit a pastry bag with the #7 plain tip and fill with icing. Keep the rest of the icing in a bowl, pressing a piece of plastic wrap against the surface to prevent it from drying out. Pipe icing along the bottom edge of the rear piece A. Position it where you want it to stand on the board and place a heavy mug or can on each side to help it stand upright until the icing dries. Pipe icing along the bottom edge and back edge of side piece B and attach it to the right side of the back so that the side edge of the side is flush against the front of the back piece. Repeat with side piece C on the left and the front piece D, adding more mugs for support as necessary. Insert straight pins through the front wall into each side wall and through the back wall into each side wall. Let stand to dry for 1 hour. Remove the mugs and pins.

10. **ATTACH THE ROOF:** Pipe icing along the top edges of the sides and the top edges of the front and back of the house. Position roof piece E on the top back of the house, lining it up so its top edge runs from point to point of the sides of the house. Secure the roof piece by inserting a straight pin through the front and back of the house and into the roof at the peak and at the eaves. Double-check that the overhang will fit in the "notched" part of the front roof piece. Rasp if necessary. Pipe icing along top of front wall and sides, set roof piece F in place, and secure with pins. Let stand until the icing is dry, about 1 hour. Remove the pins.

11. **ATTACH THE CHIMNEY:** Double-check the fit of the notched chimney piece that sits

on the roof. Rasp to fit the roof slope if necessary. Pipe icing on sides and bottom notch and glue, brick side out, to the top of the house flush with the side, inserting it into the notch cut out in the roof for it. Pipe icing along the long edges of chimney piece G and one side of each chimney piece H and I. Glue together, brick side out. Pipe icing along the long exposed edges of the chimney and attach to side of house, lining up to the notched piece. Attach the flat chimpney top with icing. Let stand to dry for 1 hour.

15. ATTACH THE OVERHANG ROOF:
Pipe icing along the edges of one of the overhang roof pieces. Position it on top of the overhang so it fits flush with the roof and overlaps the overhang. Secure with pins. Repeat with the second roof piece. Let stand to dry for 3 hours. Remove the pins.

16. DECORATE THE HOUSE: Use a small offset spatula to cover the top story of the main house and the front and sides of the overhang with white icing. Select the straightest black Twizzlers, cut to size, and press them into the icing to create the half-timbering, piping additional icing on the backs of the pieces as necessary. Cut the orange, pink, and brown licorice allsorts in half. Pipe a small dot of icing on the back of each one and glue them to the house to create the horizontal trim board all around. Repeat, creating 3 pieces of trim board on the overhang. One by one, pipe icing onto the top and back edges of the brackets and position 4 at the underside of the

12. ATTACH THE OVERHANG SIDE WALLS: Pipe icing along the back angled edges of the overhang side walls. Press into the front of the house, fitting them into each side of the notch cut out of the roof. Secure with pins and let stand to dry for 1 hour. Remove the pins.

13. ATTACH THE BACK DOOR ROOF PIECES: Pipe icing along the back edge of each back door roof piece and glue above the back door, securing with pins. Let stand to dry for 1 hour. Remove the pins.

14. ATTACH THE OVERHANG FRONT WALL: Pipe icing along the outer edges of the overhang side walls and attach the front piece to the walls. Secure with pins and place two 5¼-inch-tall drinking glasses underneath the wall to support it as the icing dries. Pipe icing along the edges of the overhang underside piece, and attach it to the underside of the overhang. Secure with pins and place 2 5¼-inch tall drinking glasses underneath the wall to support it as the icing dries. Let stand to dry for 1 hour.

one at a time, and apply a row of pieces along the bottom edge of one side of the roof, cutting the pieces at the ends of the rows to fit as necessary. Apply another row above this one, slightly overlapping it. Continue until you reach the peak of the roof, making 11 to 13 rows in total. Repeat on the other side of the roof and on the overhang roof and back door roof, cutting the shredded wheat to fit as necessary.

20. ATTACH THE PINNACLES: Pipe a dot of icing on each of 3 blue nonpareil allsorts and place 1 each on the roof pinnacle, the overhang pinnacle, and the back door pinnacle. Pipe a dot of icing onto the bottom of each of 3 black licorice allsorts men and attach one to each pinnacle.

21. MAKE THE CHIMNEY POTS AND FLUES: Remove the black centers of 3 bull's-eye allsorts. Break the candy sticks into 3-inch lengths and insert 3 of them into the allsorts. Glue the chimney pots with flues on top of the chimney.

overhang and 2 under the back door roof pieces. Secure with pins and let dry for 1½ hours.

17. LAY THE WALKWAYS AND ATTACH THE DOORS: Pipe icing onto the back side of the front and back doors. Place in position, and let dry. Spread a thin layer of icing on the board in front of each doorway. Arrange the black-and-white-and-yellow striped allsorts in a pattern in front of the front entry and the back entry. Pipe icing along the bottom edge and back edges of each door and attach to the doorways.

18. TRIM THE WINDOWS AND DOORS: Spoon about ⅓ cup icing into a small bowl and tint with 1 drop of blue food coloring. Scrape the icing into a pastry bag fitted with a #47 basket-weave tip and use the plain side to pipe the blue icing around each window and around the doors. Pipe another rectangle of icing decoratively around the door.

19. SHINGLE THE ROOF WITH SHREDDED WHEAT: Squeeze a little bit of white icing on the shredded wheat pieces,

22. ATTACH THE WREATH: Pipe a small dot of icing onto the backs of 3 blue and 3 pink nonpareil allsorts and glue them, alternating colors, in a circle between the front door and lower front window. Cut thin slices from a ridged black allsort to create 6 small black flowers and attach between the pink and blue allsorts.

23. LANDSCAPE THE HOUSE: Use a large offset spatula to spread a thin layer of icing in front of the house and to the edge of the board, to resemble a snow-covered yard. Glue together 3 yellow-and-black round allsorts on each side of the walkway to create the short entry pillars. Glue the marsh-mallows in a row at the edge of the board to create the hedge and pipe a pink or yellow bow on each one if you like.

SOUTH BEACH ART DECO HOUSE

SEE TEMPLATES ON PAGE 133

INGREDIENTS

1½ RECIPES GINGERBREAD DOUGH (PAGE 83), CHILLED

2 RECIPES ROYAL ICING (PAGE 84)

6 PIECES CLEAR SHEET GELATIN WITH CROSS-HATCHING

PINK, YELLOW, VIOLET, GREEN, AND BLACK FOOD COLORING

2 DARK-COLORED NONPAREILS

½ TEASPOON BLACK SANDING SUGAR

1 .75-OUNCE POUCH RED FRUIT ROLL-UPS

ABOUT 50 GREEN AND 50 YELLOW NECCO WAFERS (FROM ABOUT 10 2.02-OUNCE PACKAGES)

1 2-OUNCE ROLL PINK BUBBLE TAPE

17 PINK WINTERGREEN CANDIES (FROM 1 7-OUNCE PACKAGE)

1 GREEN TWIZZLER, THINLY SLICED CROSSWISE INTO 6 PIECES

3 MILK DUDS

2 .75-OUNCE POUCHES GREEN FRUIT ROLL-UPS

Our gingerbread art deco bungalow exhibits some of the style's most amusing details. The ROUNDED CORNER of the house is created by forming small pieces of gingerbread over empty aluminum cans before baking. The THREE-STEP TRIM above the door is characteristic of Miami art deco style and also a bit like a Christmas tree. The STARFISH MOTIF at the top of the house is both an allusion to warm waters and a nod to the holiday. Windows are trimmed with gray icing that mimics the METAL first used in windows during the period. A PALM TREE (with fronds made from fruit leather and Milk Dud coconuts) and PINK FLAMINGO cookies decorate the site.

CONSTRUCTION NOTES

The most challenging element of this otherwise simple house is baking the pieces for the curved front corner and putting them together. The aluminum cans that give the pieces their rounded shape tend to roll around on the baking sheet as you move it in and out of the oven. Take care to prevent this so your carefully arranged dough doesn't slide off the cans at any stage and become misshapen. Once you have successfully baked the pieces, let them cool completely on the cans so they maintain their shape.

While sheet gelatin makes great window glass in any of our houses, here it is a necessity to create the curved windows that give the house its art deco character. Glue the sheet gelatin securely to the inside of the house before attaching the roof and window grates.

If your brand of fruit leather is very soft or your kitchen is very humid, your palm fronds may flop over instead of standing straight out from the trunk. If this is the case, you can use icing to glue small lengths of spaghetti underneath the fronds to give them shape.

SPECIAL EQUIPMENT

12 x 18-INCH CUTTING BOARD OR FOIL-COVERED STYROFOAM BOARD

2 EMPTY 6-OUNCE ALUMINUM CANS, LABELS REMOVED

1 1-INCH STAR COOKIE CUTTER

PASTRY BAGS AND #7 PLAIN TIP AND #2 PLAIN TIP

HISTORICAL NOTE

The art deco style of the 1920s drew inspiration from a variety of disparate movements and events. Cubism contributed to the boxy shapes. Idealization of machines is evidenced in the sleek, rounded edges of the buildings and the horizontal lines of windows and railings, all suggesting awareness of aerodynamics. Decorative facades paid tribute to the ancient art of Egypt and the recent discovery of Tutankhamen's tomb. In Miami, art deco bungalows exhibited these traits plus regional details such as bright pastel colors and nautical round windows.

more south beach art deco style

Our version of a South Beach bungalow uses regional, nautical decorative elements. To make it more exotic and glittering, consider adding the following:

- Egyptian, Assyrian, or Persian geometrical trim. A more complex geometric design could be substituted for the simple row of starfish that rings the house near the roof.

- Modern metalwork. Aluminum, stainless steel, and bronze were used decoratively as well as functionally in art deco buildings. Use edible gold and silver dragées, gold and silver edible glitter, and gold-covered Jordan almonds (see Resources, page 86) anywhere on the house instead of gray icing and anywhere else metal might have been used, such as hardware and decorative trim.

1. BAKE THE GINGERBREAD: Enlarge the templates on pieces of thin cardboard or sturdy paper and cut to size. Preheat the oven to 375°F.

2. Divide the dough into 5 equal pieces. Wrap 4 pieces tightly in plastic wrap and keep in the refrigerator. Lightly flour a piece of parchment paper and roll out the fifth piece of dough onto the parchment so it is ¼ inch thick. Place the template for the front of the house on the dough and cut around the template with a sharp knife. Cut away the door opening and set aside the door piece. Cut away the windows. Remove the scraps from the parchment, wrap them in plastic, and refrigerate until ready to reroll.

3. Slide the parchment onto a rimless baking sheet. Place the door piece next to the front piece on the baking sheet, at least 1 inch away from it. Slide the baking sheet into the oven and bake until the door is firm, about 10 minutes. Use a metal spatula to remove the door to a wire rack to cool. Continue to bake the front piece until the edges are lightly browned and the center is firm, 2 to 4 minutes more. Slide the parchment onto a wire rack and let cool completely.

4. Working in 4 batches and using the remaining 4 pieces of dough, repeat the rolling and baking with the rear piece and door, side pieces, roof, terrace floor, and terrace wall pieces.

5. Place the aluminum cans on a baking sheet and steady them by pressing pieces of gingerbread dough between the cans and the baking sheet on either side of each can. Roll out the remaining gingerbread scraps on parchment paper and cut the 3 side curve pieces with a sharp knife. Use scissors to cut the parchment around the pieces, leaving about ½ inch

of paper exposed. Drape the 2 smaller pieces, with the underlying parchment, over one of the cans and gently mold them to the curve of the can. Drape the largest piece over the other can, molding in the same way. Bake until firm, about 10 minutes. Transfer the baking sheet to a wire rack and let the curved pieces cool on top of the cans.

6. FORM AND BAKE THE PALM TREE TRUNK: Form a leftover piece of gingerbread into a tree trunk shape about 6 inches long and 1 inch thick, making its base a little thicker. Score horizontally with the dull edge of a paring knife to create the palm tree bark. Bake on a parchment-lined baking sheet until firm, about 18 minutes.

7. CUT AND BAKE THE FLAMINGOS, STAR TRIM, AND TRIM ABOVE DOOR: Roll out some leftover dough and cut out two flamingos using the templates. Using a star-shaped cookie cutter, cut twenty-one 1-inch stars. Cut out 3 above-door trim pieces using the template. Bake on a parchment-lined baking sheet until firm, about 10 minutes.

8. When the pieces are cool, transfer the flat ones to baking sheets. Tightly cover all of the sheets in plastic until you are ready to assemble the house. They will keep for up to 1 week.

9. ASSEMBLE THE HOUSE: If you are illuminating your house, see page 13. Fit a pastry bag with the #7 plain tip and fill with icing. Keep the rest of the icing in a bowl, pressing a piece of plastic wrap against the surface to prevent it from drying out. Pipe icing along the bottom edge of the rear piece A. Position it where you want it to stand on the board and place a heavy mug or can on each side to help it stand upright until the icing dries. Pipe icing along the bottom edge and back edge of piece B and attach to the left side of the rear facade so the edge of the side is flush against the front of the rear facade piece. Repeat with the side piece C on the right side, adding more mugs for support as necessary. Insert straight pins through the back wall into each side wall. Wrap the tip of the pastry bag with plastic wrap and refrigerate until ready to continue. Let stand until the icing is dry, about 1 hour. Remove the mugs and pins.

10. ATTACH THE FRONT: Pipe icing along the bottom edge and the shorter side edge of the front facade, piece D, and attach to the terrace side of the house so the side edge of the front piece is flush against the side edge of the side piece. Insert straight pins through the front wall and into the side wall. Let stand until the icing is dry, about 1 hour. Remove the pins.

11. ATTACH THE CURVED CORNER PIECES: Pipe icing on the bottom and along the side edges of the bottom curved piece and fit it snugly between the side wall and the front facade. Repeat with the middle curved piece, inserting a straight pin through the front wall

into the curved piece to keep it in place. Repeat with the top curved piece, also inserting a pin through the front wall and into the curved piece to keep it in place. Let stand to dry for 1 hour. Remove the pins.

12. ATTACH THE WINDOW GLASS: Cut the sheet gelatin so it is ½ inch larger all around than the windows. Attach the sheets to the inside of the house with icing. The two large pieces should follow the curves of the house. The smaller pieces will lie flat.

13. ATTACH THE TERRACE FLOOR AND WALLS: Pipe icing along the underside edges of the terrace floor piece and set

it into place. Secure it to the front and side of the house with straight pins and let stand to dry for 1 hour. Pipe icing along the edges of the terrace wall pieces and fit them into place, securing with pins as necessary. Let stand to dry for 1 hour. Remove the pins.

14. ATTACH THE LARGE ROOF PIECE: Pipe icing onto the underside edges of the large roof piece and set it on top of the house. Let stand to dry for 1 hour.

15. DECORATE THE FLAMINGOS: While the house is drying, put 2 tablespoons icing in a small bowl and use a little bit of pink food coloring to tint the icing bright pink. Use the flat side of a paring knife to spread the icing over the gingerbread flamingos. Use tweezers to place a nonpareil on each head to create an eye. Sprinkle black sanding sugar on the tip of the beaks to color them black. Cut 2 small triangles from the Fruit Roll-Ups. Pipe a dot at one tip of each triangle and a stripe on the opposite side to create the Santa hats. Let dry for 1 hour.

16. COLOR THE STARS: Place 1 teaspoon icing in a small bowl and use a drop of yellow food coloring to make it yellow. Spread the yellow icing over the top of one of the ginger-

bread stars. Spoon $\frac{1}{4}$ cup frosting into another small bowl and use a drop of violet food coloring to make it pale purple. Spread the purple icing over the tops of the remaining star cookies. Let the cookies dry for 1 hour.

17. STUCCO THE HOUSE: Meanwhile, put $3\frac{1}{2}$ cups icing in a medium bowl and use 2 to 3 drops of green food coloring to tint the icing pale green. Smooth the icing over the roof, front, back, terrace walls, and sides to cover the gingerbread completely. Let stand to dry for 1 hour.

18. PIPE THE METAL WINDOW FRAMES: Put $\frac{1}{2}$ cup icing in a small bowl and use a little bit of black food coloring to tint it gray. Scrape into a pastry bag fitted with the #2 plain tip and pipe icing along the edges of the windows to create metal window frames. Cover the tip of the pastry bag with plastic wrap and refrigerate. Let dry for 1 hour.

19. COLOR THE DOORS AND TRIM ABOVE DOOR: Mix 3 tablespoons icing with a couple of drops of green food coloring and a little bit of black to create a dark jade green. Spread some of this icing over each door. Pipe a dot of the gray icing on each door for a doorknob. Pipe gray icing around the round window of the front door. Spread some of the dark green icing on one side of each half-circle of trim above door piece. Let dry for 1 hour.

20. LAY THE TILE: Use a small spatula to spread white icing all around the house. Lay the Necco wafers in rows, alternating yellow and green, all around the house, breaking them to fit as necessary. Let dry for 1 hour.

21. ATTACH THE WINDOW GRATES: Unroll the bubble gum and use a sharp paring knife to cut 4 pieces measuring $6\frac{1}{4}$ x $\frac{1}{16}$ inch. Cut 20 pieces measuring $3\frac{1}{2}$ x $\frac{1}{16}$ inch. Cut

10 pieces measuring 3 x ⅟₁₆ inch. Cut 8 pieces measuring 2¼ x ⅟₁₆ inch. Pipe a small dot of icing on each end of each 3½-inch strip. Glue 5 of these vertically over each of the large curved windows, spacing them evenly. Glue 2 of them vertically over the lower front and side windows. Glue 1 each vertically over the remaining windows. Pipe small dots of icing on each end of the 6¼-inch pieces and pipe small dots of icing on the vertical pieces placed over the curving windows where the horizontal grates will be placed. Glue the 6¼-inch pieces over the curving windows horizontally, fixing them to each side of the window with the icing and attaching them to the vertical grates where you have piped the icing. Repeat with the remaining strips, gluing them horizontally onto the remaining windows, using the 3-inch strips on the rear facade windows and the window above the front door and the 2¼-inch strips on the small side windows and on the lower front and side windows that are not curved.

22. **MAKE THE TERRACE RAILING:** Cut four 2½-inch strips of bubble gum. Using icing, glue 5 wintergreen candies along the edge of the terrace, spacing them evenly along the front and side. Glue a strip of bubble gum on top of the front row of candies and on top of the side row of candies. Glue another 5 candies on top of the first candies and the strips of gum. Repeat with the remaining gum strips and 5 more candies.

23. **ATTACH THE DOORS:** Attach the front and back doors to the house with icing.

24. **ATTACH THE DRAINAGE SPOUTS:** Pipe icing onto one side of each Twizzler piece. Glue 3 pieces in a row about 1 inch below the roof on the back wall of the terrace. Glue the remaining 3 pieces in a row about 1 inch below the roof on the rear facade above the top left window.

25. **ATTACH THE TRIM ABOVE THE DOOR:** Pipe icing onto the straight edge of each above-door trim piece and attach above the door, largest on bottom and smallest on top, securing each piece with a straight pin.

26. **ATTACH THE STAR BORDER:** Pipe icing onto the back of the yellow star and glue it above the center front window. Glue the remaining violet cookies in a row all around the house, 1 inch below the roof, skipping the sections with the drainage spouts.

27. **PLACE THE FLAMINGOS AND PALM TREE:** Using icing, glue 2 pink wintergreen candies to the Necco tiles between the curved window and the front door. Pipe a little bit of icing in front of each candy and place a flamingo on top of the icing, using the wintergreen candies as supports. Pipe a little bit of icing on the top of each flamingo's head and glue a Santa hat to each flamingo. Pipe a little icing on the Necco tiles on the other side of the door. Use a serrated knife to cut a little bit of the thick end off of the palm tree trunk, so the end is flat, and glue it to the tiles. Glue 3 Milk Duds onto the trunk, close to the top. Fold the green Fruit Roll-Up into a double thickness and then use a paring knife to cut palm fronds measuring 4 x ¾ inch. Use the knife to make tiny cuts on each side of each frond. Glue the fronds to the top of the trunk, securing with straight pins until dry, about 1 hour. Remove the pins.

MODERN HOUSE

SEE TEMPLATES ON PAGE 137

Our modern gingerbread house has SHARP, ANGULAR LINES, a flat roof, and large glass panel windows. Smooth fondant stands in for STUCCOED CONCRETE. Red, green, and yellow Haribo Brixx make a colorful geometric paved pathway. A ZEN SAND GARDEN made with turbinado sugar can be raked into varying designs while the house is on display. Two simply frosted ice cream cone trees and three jelly ring wreaths add to the geometric look.

special equipment

12 x 18-INCH CUTTING BOARD OR FOIL-COVERED STYROFOAM BOARD

PASTRY BAG AND #7 PLAIN TIP

INGREDIENTS

2 RECIPES GINGER-BREAD DOUGH (PAGE 83), CHILLED

2 1-POUND BAGS CLEAR HARD CANDIES, CRUSHED IN A FOOD PROCESSOR

16 PIECES LINGUINE

BLACK, GREEN, RED, AND VIOLET FOOD COLORING

1½ RECIPES ROYAL ICING (PAGE 84)

2 ICE CREAM SUGAR CONES

6 4-INCH PRETZEL STICKS

4½ POUNDS FONDANT (SEE RESOURCES, PAGE 86)

CONFECTIONERS' SUGAR

4 OUNCES RED SANDING SUGAR

3 STUBBY PIECES BLACK LICORICE

3 OBLONG SILVER DRAGÉES

1 .75-OUNCE POUCH RED FRUIT ROLL-UPS

3 GREEN JELLY RINGS

ABOUT 75 YELLOW, RED, AND GREEN HARIBO BRIXX GUMMY CANDIES (FROM 2 5-OUNCE BAGS)

½ CUP SWEETENED FLAKED COCONUT

2 TO 3 TABLESPOONS TURBINADO SUGAR, SUCH AS SUGAR IN THE RAW

CONSTRUCTION NOTES

This house has large panels of glass, both attached to the gingerbread walls and free-floating. Because they are so big, they must be thicker and less fragile than the candy glass windows in the other houses. Unlit, the windows are quite opaque, so look for hard candy that is pale (we used clear hard candies rather than butterscotch) for the most translucent look. We call for quite a lot of candy, so you'll have extra on hand if you need to redo any of your windows.

Although our other gingerbread houses don't have floors, this one does, to help support the glass and gingerbread panels.

German architects of the Bauhaus movement in the first decades of the twentieth century set out to design housing for workers that was functional but beautiful, without "bourgeois" details like cornices, trim, and other ornamentation. In the 1920s and '30s, the style was adapted by American architects such as Philip Johnson and Richard Neutra, who built simple but luxurious homes with flat roofs, smooth facades, and open floor plans made up of cubic shapes for their wealthy clients.

more modern style

It is possible to embellish the Modern house and still be true to its minimalist aesthetic. Here are a couple of ideas:

- We can imagine candy bonsai trees decorating the site.

- A rake made out of pastillage, for making designs in the sand garden, would be both useful and pretty.

1. BAKE THE GINGERBREAD: Enlarge the templates on pieces of thin cardboard or sturdy paper and cut to size. Preheat the oven to 375°F.

2. Divide the dough into 5 equal pieces. Wrap 4 pieces tightly in plastic wrap and keep in the refrigerator. Lightly flour a piece of parchment paper and roll out the fifth piece of the dough on the parchment so it is ¼ inch thick. Place the templates for the front facade piece A, the door, and the green entry wall piece on the dough and cut around the templates with a sharp knife. Remove the scraps from the parchment, wrap in plastic, and refrigerate until ready to reroll.

3. Slide the parchment onto a rimless baking sheet. Slide the baking sheet into the oven. Bake front facade piece A, the door, and the green entry wall until the edges are lightly browned and the center is firm, 10 minutes for the door, 12 to 14 minutes for the front and wall. Remove from the oven and let cool on the pan for 5 minutes.

4. Sprinkle a thick layer of crushed candy into the 2 spaces cut away from the right-hand side of the front facade for glass. (The opening at the bottom left will be filled in by the front door.) Straighten the edges with the edge of a knife (the candy may spread during baking). Return the baking sheet to the oven until the candy is melted, 5 to 7 minutes. Check the candy during baking and if necessary carefully straighten the molten candy with the edge of a knife or a metal ruler. Remove from the oven. If the side of the candy glass not bordered by gingerbread has spread or is not completely straight, let it cool slightly so it is solid but still pliable, and then use the edge of a knife to straighten the edge. Let the gingerbread cool completely before sliding the pieces, still on the parchment, off the pan and continuing.

5. Working in 3 batches and using 3 of the remaining pieces of dough plus scraps, repeat the rolling and baking with the second floor, supporting wall piece D, and 2 side pieces B and C, adding window glass to all the openings of piece C, and baking again until melted.

6. Roll out the remaining piece of dough and cut both roof pieces, the floating front wall, and the floor and roof support pieces. Bake until firm, 12 to 14 minutes. Slide the parchment onto a wire rack, and let cool completely.

7. When the pieces are cool, transfer them to baking sheets and tightly cover the sheets in plastic until you are ready to assemble the house. They will keep for up to 1 week.

8. BAKE THE GLASS PANELS: Line a baking sheet with parchment paper and spread crushed hard candy into a rectangle measuring 7 x 11 inches and ½ inch thick. Straighten the edges with the back of a knife. Bake until the candy has melted into a smooth sheet, about 6 minutes, checking every 2 minutes to make sure it is not burning. Remove the baking sheet from the oven and

let cool until the candy is still warm and pliable but has begun to solidify, 2 to 3 minutes. Use the edge of a metal ruler or a knife to score the candy glass, making 3 panels with the dimensions as shown on the plans; finesse the dimensions to fit your specific house if necessary. When the candy glass is cool, gently break the candy panel at the scored edges. If you want to alter the window after it has cooled, just warm the candy window in the oven again, then gently and carefully press the candy edge in the direction you wish with the flat edge of a knife.

9. **DYE THE LINGUINE PIECES:** Arrange the linguine on a piece of parchment paper and use a paintbrush and black food coloring to tint them black. Set aside to dry.

10. **MAKE THE FIR TREES:** Tint ¼ cup icing with green food coloring and spread it in a thin, smooth layer over the outside of the sugar cones. Let stand to dry for about 1 hour. Overturn each cone into a small cup and ice the inside of each cone with white icing. Glue the ends of 3 pretzel sticks to the interior point of each cone so they form a thick trunk extending about ½ inch from the wide edge of the cone. Let stand to dry for 1 hour.

11. **COLOR AND ATTACH THE FONDANT:** Meanwhile, tint three 1-cup portions of fondant with 6 or more drops each red, green, and violet food coloring. Keep any fondant you are not using wrapped tightly in plastic. Lightly sprinkle a work surface with confectioners' sugar and roll the red fondant to a ¼-inch thickness. Cut and glue the red fondant to the door piece. Repeat with the green piece, attaching to the entry wall and side panel. Repeat the rolling and cutting with the violet piece, attaching to the floating roof piece. Wrap the remaining violet fondant in plastic and set aside (you will use it later to trim the balcony). Cover the windows attached to the gingerbread with parchment paper. Repeat the rolling and cutting with the white fondant,

attaching it to the front, back, and sides where indicated in the photos and trimming around the windows. Wrap the remaining white fondant in plastic and set aside.

12. **ATTACH THE LINGUINE TO THE WALLS:** Set aside 3 pieces of the black linguine. Cut the remaining pasta into lengths to match the patterns on the exterior walls of the house and use a small amount of icing to glue them to the fondant-covered walls to create the black trim.

13. **ASSEMBLE THE HOUSE:** If you are illuminating your house, see page 13. Fit the pastry bag with the #7 plain tip and fill with white icing. Keep the rest of the icing in a bowl, pressing a piece of plastic wrap against the surface to prevent it from drying out. Pipe icing along the bottom edge of the front of the front facade piece A. Position it where you want it to stand on the board and place a heavy mug or can on the back side (taking care not to damage the decorated front side) to help it stand upright until the icing dries. Pipe icing along the bottom edge and front edge of side piece B and attach it to the left side of the front facade so that the side edge of the side is flush against the back of the front piece. Repeat with side piece C, attaching it to the right side of the front facade and adding more mugs for support as necessary. Insert straight pins through the side walls into the front wall. Glue the green entry wall perpendicularly onto the front facade so that the green entry extends into the main house space by 1½ inches. Glue the red door piece to the interior edge of the green entry piece and the middle of piece B. Wrap the tip of the pastry bag with plastic wrap and refrigerate until ready to continue. Let stand until the icing is dry, about 1 hour. Remove the mugs and pins.

14. Glue the 4 floor supports to the inside of the house, 2 on each side piece (these will support the second-story floor). Let stand to dry for 15 minutes. Pipe icing onto the top of each

support and on the top of the green entry wall and insert the second-story floor into the house, resting it on the supports and the green wall. Let stand to dry for 15 minutes.

15. Glue the 4 roof supports to the second-story floor and to the side pieces, 2 on each side. Glue piece *D* to the board and the second-story floor, sliding it into the notch in the second-story floor, grating the notch edge with a handheld grater or a rasp so the piece will fit, if necessary. Let stand to dry for 15 minutes.

16. ATTACH THE ROOF AND FLOATING FRONT PANEL: Test the inset roof (the main roof piece) for size by gently placing it into position; trim any uneven edges with a handheld grater or a rasp. Place the sanding sugar in a pan and gently shake to level. Ice the surface and exposed back edge of the main roof piece with red-tinted icing and place the iced side and end of the roof into the red sugar. Sprinkle the remaining red sugar over any bald spots on the roof surface, shake the excess sugar into the pan, and set aside to dry for 1 hour. Pipe icing on top of each roof support and rest the large red sugar-covered roof piece on the supports and on the balcony wall so that the roof is flush with the front facade. Pipe icing along the top edges of the 2 side walls where the violet roof piece will rest, and place that piece on top. Glue the floating front wall to the violet roof piece at the top and to the green entry wall at the bottom, so the panel is steadying the violet roof piece. Let stand to dry for 15 minutes.

17. ATTACH THE REAR GLASS PANELS: Using icing, carefully glue the 3 glass panels into place.

18. ROLL OUT AND CUT THE WINDOW TOP PARAPET AND THE WINDOW TRIM: Roll out the remaining violet fondant to a ¼-inch thickness and cut into lengths to fit the windows. Knead black food coloring into the remaining white fondant, roll out, and trim to the length of the wall. Set the trim pieces aside to dry overnight. Use white icing to glue the trim to the windows and the top of the wall.

19. ATTACH THE LINGUINE RAILINGS: Use a sharp skewer to make small holes in the balcony walls where the railings will be attached. Cut the remaining linguine to fit between the walls and glue onto the balcony, inserting the ends in the holes.

20. ATTACH THE CHIMNEYS: Glue the 3 stubby pieces of black licorice to the roof. Glue the dragées to the licorice, inserting one end into the hole in each licorice piece.

21. ATTACH THE WREATHS. Shape 3 bows from the Fruit Roll-Ups and attach 1 to each of the jelly rings. Glue the jelly ring wreaths to the floating front panel of the house.

22. LANDSCAPE THE HOUSE: Glue the Haribo Brixx to the board with white icing, making a walkway to the front door and a border for the sand garden.

23. Combine the coconut and a few drops of green food coloring in the work bowl of a food processor and pulse several times until the coconut is green. Tint 1 cup icing (or more if necessary) with green food coloring and spread it in a thin layer over the board surrounding the house, except for the defined sand garden area. Press the green coconut into the icing.

24. Stand the trees on the grass, gluing the trunks to the grass with green icing. Pour the turbinado sugar into the sand garden space and make a swirling pattern with the back of a small spoon (the sugar remains loose, so you can change this pattern at any time).

The following list is short, but everything on it is absolutely necessary for making a house:

CARDBOARD You can use a copier to enlarge templates on paper, or you can draw them on graph paper, but you'll then want to trace the paper templates onto thin cardboard so that they are sturdy enough to stay in place on top of rolled dough as you cut. Posterboard from a stationery store also works well and is big enough to accommodate even the largest templates.

CUTTING BOARD OR OTHER DISPLAY BOARD You will need a sturdy, rigid board on which to assemble your house. Large cutting boards work well, as does 1-inch-thick Styrofoam from a craft store. Choose a board at least 3 to 4 inches larger around than the footprint of your house so you will have room for landscaping.

HEAVY-DUTY STAND MIXER A heavy-duty stand mixer such as a KitchenAid is a must for making gingerbread dough. Its powerful motor can mix large batches of dough quickly and efficiently without burning out, and it whips up lots of smooth, fluffy Royal Icing in minutes. It may seem like a splurge, but it is so practical and beautifully designed that if you are like us, once you bring it home you'll wonder how you ever baked without one.

PARCHMENT PAPER Rolling dough out right onto parchment paper is the easiest way to get your gingerbread pieces from the work surface to the oven. It also makes sliding the pieces off of the baking sheets a breeze.

PARING KNIFE Cutting your dough with the tip of a sharp paring knife will give your gingerbread pieces a clean edge.

PASTRY BAGS AND TIPS You have wonderful control when you use a pastry bag and a plain tip to pipe icing onto gingerbread pieces as you put a house together. We love disposable plastic pastry bags for their convenience. Just a few plain tips and a ridged basket-weave tip will allow you to accomplish all of the piping we use to make and decorate these houses. Equipment lists preceding each recipe let you know which ones you will need for that specific house.

ROLLING PIN We use untapered rolling pins with wooden handles, but any kind of pin you already own or are comfortable with will work to roll out gingerbread dough.

RIMLESS BAKING SHEETS Rimless baking sheets are best for gingerbread because they allow you to slide gingerbread pieces on and off without lifting them, greatly reducing the chances of breaking and otherwise damaging the pieces in the process.

RULER Not only is a ruler necessary for cutting out templates but it also comes in handy for a variety of other gingerbread-related tasks, such as serving as a guide for trimming uneven pieces of gingerbread as they come out of the oven and scoring icing to create the look of siding.

SPATULAS You'll need two kinds of spatulas: a rubber one for scraping down the sides of a mixing bowl and a small offset spatula to spread icing over large areas like walls and roofs.

STRAIGHT PINS Use straight pins with big, brightly colored balls on the ends to hold together your just-glued gingerbread pieces until the icing is dry. If you don't, your pieces might shift or even fall away from each other and break before the icing has time to do its job. You can find these in craft stores or anywhere sewing supplies are sold.

TWEEZERS Use tweezers for placing small items.

X-ACTO KNIFE A razor-sharp knife with replacement blades is extremely useful for cutting templates; trimming gingerbread edges; cutting Pocky Sticks, jellybeans, and fruit leather; finessing a clear icing edge; lifting parchment paper from candy windows; and putting small candies precisely in place.

Aside from standard baking ingredients (flour, baking powder, sugar, vegetable shortening) and the entire contents of your local candy store, you will need some or all of the following to bake and decorate your house:

FONDANT A thick, creamy sugar paste, fondant can be tinted with food coloring and then rolled or shaped to create siding, moldings, and other kinds of trim and decorations. Although you can make it yourself, buying it is more convenient and ensures that it will be smooth and easy to roll and mold (see Resources, page 86). It hardens as it dries, so wrap it tightly in plastic when you aren't working with it. Fondant isn't difficult to use, but if you'd rather not give it a try on your first gingerbread house outing, it is easy to avoid. We use fondant to make the siding for the Carpenter Gothic, the Urban Brownstone, and the Modern House, which is one reason why we rate these among the most difficult houses to make. We also use it to simulate the snow-covered roof and lawn of the Victorian Farmhouse. Royal Icing piped with a pastry bag using a large basket-weave tip can stand in for the fondant trim in the first case. Royal Icing spread with a spatula over the roof and board is a good substitute in the second.

FOOD COLORING We like to custom-mix our food colors to get just the right tint, so a large set of eight or twelve colors allows us to get the Taos blue for our Pueblo House door or the jade green for the door of our South Beach Art Deco House.

MERINGUE POWDER A mixture of powdered egg whites and sugar, meringue powder is the secret ingredient in stable, superstrong icing. It is available in many supermarkets and specialty foods stores, and it can be ordered online from any baking supply house (see Resources, page 86).

MOLASSES We call for dark (not light or blackstrap) molasses in our recipes because it gives the gingerbread a good color—not too pale, not too brown—and a delicious aroma and robust sweetness.

PASTILLAGE Similar to rolled fondant, pastillage does not contain softening ingredients such as glycerin or shortening. It becomes bone dry and is perfect for small decorative elements that need to be sharp and crisp, such as the cornice and architraves on the Urban Brownstone. (Don't worry if you aren't up for making pastillage. We give suggestions for simpler ways of getting a similar effect.) Pastillage gets very hard and can even be smoothed and sanded with a handheld grater, a rasp, or sandpaper. Keep it tightly covered in plastic wrap when you are not working with it. Knead in food coloring as necessary and let cut pieces of pastillage dry overnight before gluing them to your house. While you can buy it at a specialty store (see Resources, page 86), it is simple to make at home. We've provided the recipe we use (page 85) in case you'd like to try it. It is optional, but fun, to mold pastillage into poinsettias for the Urban Brownstone or a rake for the Modern House's sand garden.

SHEET GELATIN Gelatin that comes in sheets looks like cellophane and makes unbeatable edible window glass for gingerbread houses. Most supermarkets only carry powdered gelatin, so you may have to seek out sheet gelatin at a baking supply store or order it by mail (see Resources, page 86). We use it in the Carpenter Gothic and the Tudor Revival because it has cross-hatching that resembles the diamond-paned glass often used on those types of houses. You can always skip the gelatin on these houses and instead glue thin-cut strips of chewing gum diagonally across each window on the inside to create the same look (see the chewing-gum mullions on the Greek Revival Antebellum Plantation to get an idea of this technique). There really is no edible substitute for sheet gelatin in the case of the South Beach Art Deco House, where it simulates curved glass. But if it's easier for you to use thin, flexible clear plastic (the kind sold at office supply stores for covering children's book reports), we won't tell.

THE RECIPES

GINGERBREAD DOUGH

A large stand mixer, like the KitchenAid (see Resources, page 86), accommodates one batch of dough. If you are using a smaller, less powerful mixer, you will have to make two half recipes (below).

1 CUP VEGETABLE SHORTENING

1 CUP SUGAR

2 TEASPOONS BAKING POWDER

2 TEASPOONS GROUND GINGER

1 TEASPOON BAKING SODA

1 TEASPOON SALT

1 TEASPOON GROUND CINNAMON

1/2 TEASPOON GROUND CLOVES

1 CUP DARK (NOT LIGHT OR BLACKSTRAP) MOLASSES

2 LARGE EGGS

2 TABLESPOONS WHITE VINEGAR

5 CUPS UNBLEACHED ALL-PURPOSE FLOUR

MAKES ABOUT 3½ POUNDS

1. In the bowl of a large stand mixer fitted with the paddle attachment, combine the shortening and sugar with an electric mixer on medium-high speed until well combined.

2. Add the baking powder, ginger, baking soda, salt, cinnamon, and cloves and beat until incorporated.

3. Add the molasses, eggs, and vinegar and beat until smooth, scraping down the sides of the bowl once or twice as necessary.

4. Add the flour, 1 cup at a time, and mix on low until smooth. Scrape the dough onto a sheet of plastic wrap and press into a rough square. Wrap tightly and refrigerate for at least 3 hours and up to 3 days.

HALF-RECIPE GINGERBREAD DOUGH

Sometimes a gingerbread house requires 1½ recipes of dough. We've done the math, dividing the ingredients for the half-recipe, so you don't have to.

1/2 CUP VEGETABLE SHORTENING

1/2 CUP SUGAR

1 TEASPOON BAKING POWDER

1 TEASPOON GROUND GINGER

1/2 TEASPOON BAKING SODA

1/2 TEASPOON SALT

1/2 TEASPOON GROUND CINNAMON

1/4 TEASPOON GROUND CLOVES

1/2 CUP DARK (NOT LIGHT OR BLACKSTRAP) MOLASSES

1 LARGE EGG

1 TABLESPOON WHITE VINEGAR

2 1/2 CUPS UNBLEACHED ALL-PURPOSE FLOUR

MAKES ABOUT 1¾ POUNDS

Proceed as for full recipe.

ROYAL ICING

Meringue powder, a combination of dried egg whites and sugar, makes this icing easy to work with and gives it powerful bonding capability. In addition to serving as edible glue, Royal Icing is essential for decorating your gingerbread house. Spread over the board, it becomes snow; piped around windows, it stands in for trim; tinted and spread on top of gingerbread doors, it is colorful paint. Keep leftover icing in the refrigerator, the surface covered with plastic to prevent it from drying out, and use it for touch-ups and repairs in the days leading up to and after the holiday.

If you need two recipes' worth of icing for a house, don't try to double the ingredients and make the larger quantity all at once. Incorporating more than 4½ cups of confectioners' sugar into a standard-size bowl may create a messy snowstorm in your kitchen! Instead, make the recipe twice, transferring the first batch to another bowl and covering the surface with plastic wrap before starting again.

3 TABLESPOONS MERINGUE
POWDER

½ CUP WARM WATER

1 16-OUNCE PACKAGE
CONFECTIONERS' SUGAR (4½
CUPS)

1 TEASPOON PURE VANILLA
EXTRACT

MAKES ABOUT 6½ CUPS

1. In a medium mixing bowl, combine the meringue powder and water. With an electric mixer fitted with the whisk attachment, beat the mixture on high speed until soft peaks form.

2. Add the confectioners' sugar and vanilla and beat until the icing is shiny, smooth, and increased in volume, 6 to 8 minutes. If the icing is too stiff to pipe or spread, add 1 to 2 tablespoons water and whip until the proper consistency is achieved. Use immediately or cover the surface of the icing with plastic wrap (otherwise the icing will begin to harden) and refrigerate the bowl for up to 1 day.

HALF-RECIPE ROYAL ICING

Sometimes you'll need a half batch of icing (if your house requires 1½ batches, or if you've placed it on an extra-large board and want a big, snowy landscape). Here are the ingredient measurements for that extra half batch.

1½ TABLESPOONS
MERINGUE POWDER

¼ CUP WARM WATER

2¼ CUPS CONFECTIONERS'
SUGAR

½ TEASPOON PURE
VANILLA EXTRACT

MAKES ABOUT 3¼ CUPS

Proceed as for full recipe.

PASTILLAGE

We fell in love with this sugar paste, which is easy to make and work with. It is very good for doors and moldings because its edges are so crisp and sharp. Gum tragacanth is a natural emulsifier and thickener, available at cake supply stores (see Resources, page 86).

1 LARGE EGG WHITE

2½ CUPS CONFECTIONERS' SUGAR

2 TEASPOONS GUM TRAGACANTH

MAKES ABOUT ¾ CUP

1. In the bowl of a stand mixer fitted with the whisk attachment, beat the egg white on medium speed until it becomes foamy. Switch to the paddle attachment, add the confectioners' sugar, ½ cup at a time, and mix on low speed until the ingredients come together into a ball.

2. Add the gum tragacanth and mix on low speed until incorporated. Continue to mix until the pastillage is a stiff but smooth paste.

3. Wrap tightly in 2 layers of plastic wrap and store in a ziplock bag or an airtight container in the refrigerator for up to 1 month.

Leftover Gingerbread Dough

Our recipes call for plenty of dough so that you won't have to worry about running out just as you are rolling out the final piece of your house. Sometimes, depending on the house you choose and how thin you roll your dough, you will have a substantial amount left over—½ pound or even more. Once your house is assembled, you can use the extra dough to make gingerbread men to hang on your Christmas tree.

GINGERBREAD MEN ORNAMENTS

MAKES FIVE 5-INCH COOKIES

½ POUND LEFTOVER GINGERBREAD DOUGH (PAGE 83)

RAISINS, CHOCOLATE CHIPS, DRAGÉES, AND/OR CINNAMON RED HOTS, FOR EYES, NOSE, MOUTH, AND BUTTONS

ROYAL ICING (OPPOSITE; OPTIONAL)

1. Preheat the oven to 375°F. Line a baking sheet with parchment paper.

2. Roll out the dough on a lightly floured work surface to a ¼-inch thickness. Use a 5-inch gingerbread man cookie cutter to cut the dough, rerolling and cutting the scraps. Place the cookies on the baking sheet. Make eyes, nose, mouth, and buttons by pressing raisins, chocolate chips, dragées, or Red Hots into the cookies. Cut out a hole at the top of each cookie with a drinking straw.

3. Bake the cookies until they are firm, 8 to 10 minutes. Transfer to a wire rack and let cool completely. Decorate with the icing if desired. When the icing is completely dry, thread a 6-inch length of ribbon through each hole and knot. Gingerbread men will keep at room temperature for several weeks.

RESOURCES

Most of the equipment and ingredients you will need to create the houses in this book are available at supermarkets, candy stores, and cookware shops. A few of them, however, are not always stocked locally, in which case you can simply order online or by phone from one of the sources listed below.

CANDY CRATE

1-866-4CANDY9
www.candycrate.com

An online source for rock candy, ribbon lollipops, bulk licorice in every shape and size, gum, and every other imaginable type of candy.

CANDY DIRECT, INC.

745 Design Court, Suite 602
Chula Vista, CA 91911
619-216-0116
www.candydirect.com

Browse their inventory for French burnt peanuts, Jordan almonds, a huge selection of licorice and gum, and much more.

CANDYWAREHOUSE.COM, INC.

5314 Third Street
Irwindale, CA 91706-2060
626-480-0899
www.candywarehouse.com

This online candy store has a terrific feature for the gingerbread house builder: You can search candy by color.

DYLAN'S CANDY BAR

1011 Third Avenue
New York, NY 10021
646-735-0078
and other locations in New York, Texas, and Florida
www.dylanscandybar.com

The online store has the same well-edited selection of candy as do the colorful shops.

I LOVE SWEET TREATS

1739 Maybank Highway
Charleston, SC 29412
843-572-8500
www.ilovesweettreats.com

Based in Charleston, South Carolina, this candy source is especially well stocked with gummy candies such as sugared Power Belts, jelly rings, Sour Patch green apples, and many more. They also stock chocolate rocks.

KING ARTHUR FLOUR COMPANY

The Baker's Catalogue
58 Billings Farm Road
White River Junction, VT 05001
Norwich, VT 05055-0876
800-827-6836
www.bakerscatalogue.com

You can find almost everything you need to make a gingerbread house in the Baker's Catalogue. The large and reasonably priced selection of equipment and ingredients includes KitchenAid mixers, baking sheets, pastry bags and tips, rolling pins, and parchment paper. Ingredients your supermarket may not stock, including meringue powder and professional-quality food coloring, may also be found here.

NEW YORK CAKE SUPPLIES

56 West 22nd Street
New York, NY 10010
800-942-2539
212-675-2253
www.nycake.com

This store specializes in professional-quality ingredients and equipment, including baking sheets, parchment paper, rolling pins, fondant and fondant cutters, food coloring, meringue powder, edible gold luster dust, edible glitter, candy pebbles, and many more items to stimulate the gingerbread house maker's imagination.

SUGARCRAFT

2715 Dixie Highway
Hamilton, OH 45015
513-896-7098
www.sugarcraft.com

This is a great baking and candy-making resource, with a variety of items perfect for house-building, including light sets, Styrofoam boards and cake drums, and sheet gelatin for windows. This is our source for the edible rice paper (sometimes called wafer paper) we use to make curtains as well as gum tragacanth for pastillage.

SWEET FACTORY

Locations around the country
877-817-9338
www.sweetfactory.com

This chain of mall candy stores has a large selection, organized by color, including Power Belts in every shade, sour Licorice Stix, Candy Blox, and other hard-to-find items.

WILTON INDUSTRIES

2240 West 75th Street
Woodridge, IL 60517-0750
800-794-5866
www.wilton.com

Wilton sells decorating supplies such as pastry bags and tips, fondant and fondant cutters, and food coloring. Its website offers detailed instructions for using a pastry bag and tips to decorate your houses.

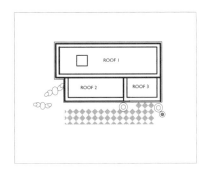

FINISHED VIEW

SITE WORKS

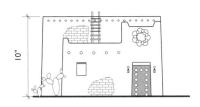

ELEVATION—FRONT FACADE

ELEVATION—SIDE FACADE

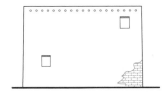

ELEVATION—REAR FACADE

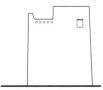

ELEVATION—SIDE FACADE

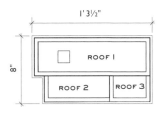

FLOOR PLAN

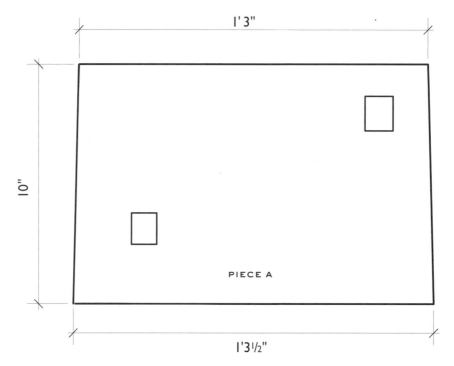

1' 3"

10"

PIECE A

1'3½"

REAR FACADE TEMPLATE

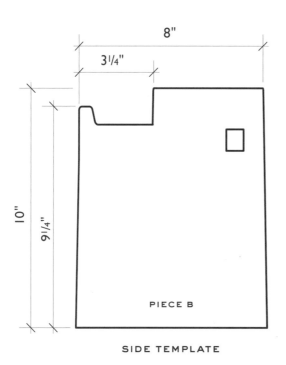

8"

3¼"

10"

9¼"

PIECE B

SIDE TEMPLATE

3¼"

PIECE G

4⅛"

3⅜"

DOOR

SIDE TEMPLATE

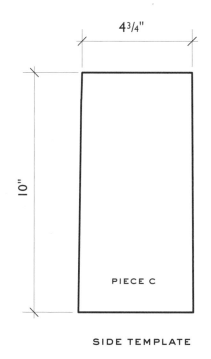

4³/₄"

10"

PIECE C

SIDE TEMPLATE

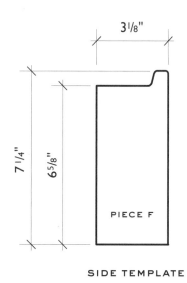

3¹/₈"

7¹/₄"

6⁵/₈"

PIECE F

SIDE TEMPLATE

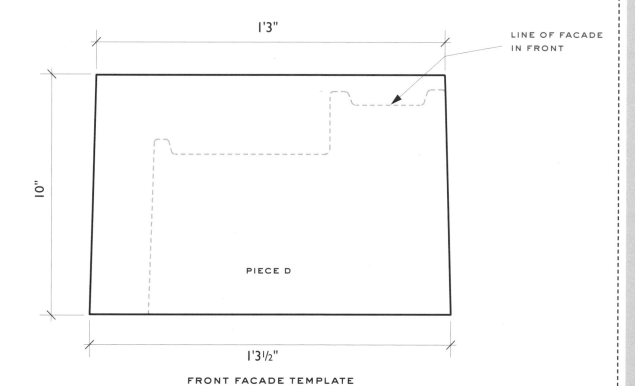

1'3"

LINE OF FACADE
IN FRONT

10"

PIECE D

1'3¹/₂"

FRONT FACADE TEMPLATE

LINE OF WALL BEYOND

1'1"

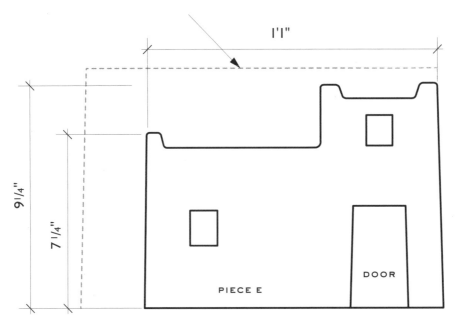

9 1/4"

7 1/4"

PIECE E

DOOR

FRONT FACADE TEMPLATE

1'2 1/2"

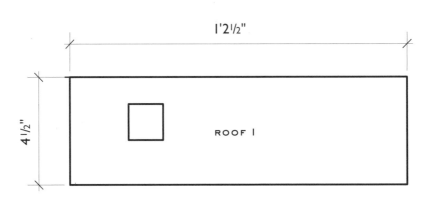

4 1/2"

ROOF 1

ROOF TEMPLATE

7 3/4"

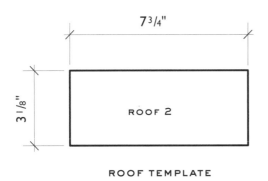

3 1/8"

ROOF 2

ROOF TEMPLATE

5"

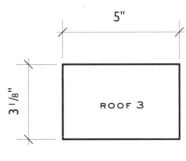

3 1/8"

ROOF 3

ROOF TEMPLATE

FINISHED VIEW

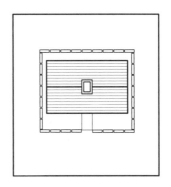

SITE WORKS

ELEVATION—FRONT FACADE

ELEVATION—SIDE FACADE

ELEVATION—REAR FACADE

ELEVATION—SIDE FACADE

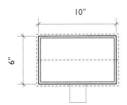

FLOOR PLAN

ROOF PLAN

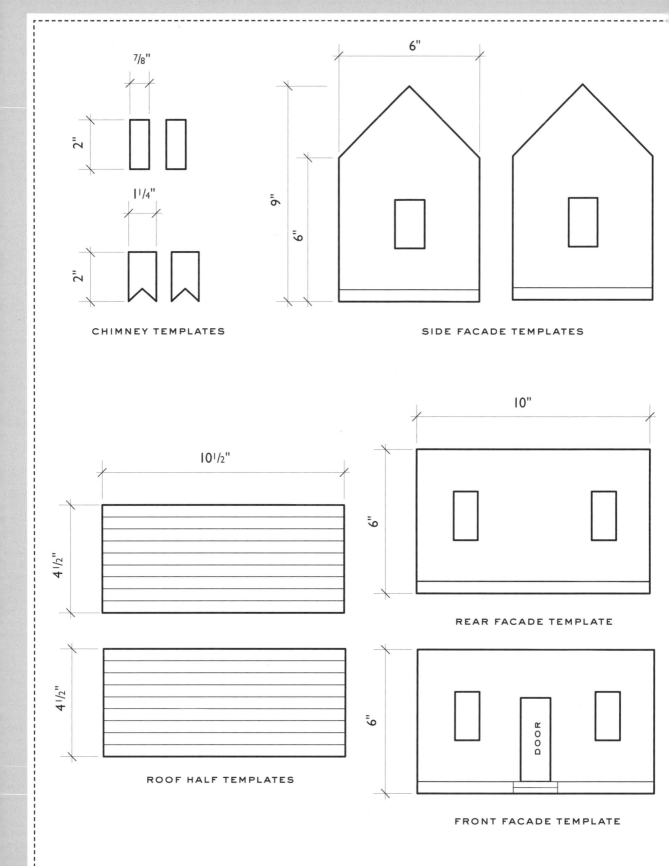

7/8"

2"

CHIMNEY TEMPLATES

1 1/4"

2"

6"

9"

6"

SIDE FACADE TEMPLATES

10 1/2"

4 1/2"

4 1/2"

ROOF HALF TEMPLATES

10"

6"

REAR FACADE TEMPLATE

6"

DOOR

FRONT FACADE TEMPLATE

FINISHED VIEW

SITE WORKS

ELEVATION—FRONT FACADE

ELEVATION—SIDE FACADE

ELEVATION—REAR FACADE

ELEVATION—SIDE FACADE

GINGERBREAD
INTERIOR
SUPPORT PIECE
FOR FRONT
EDGE OF ROOF

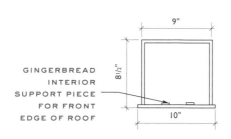

FLOOR PLAN

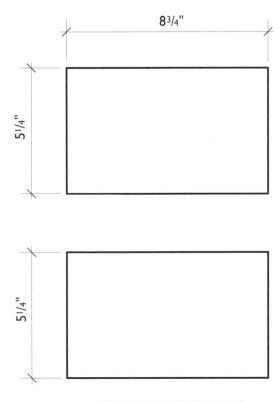

8 3/4"

5 1/4"

5 1/4"

ROOF HALF TEMPLATES

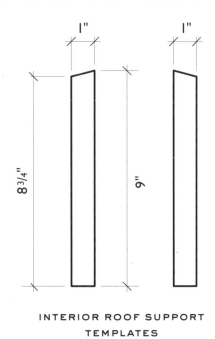

1" 1"

8 3/4" 9"

INTERIOR ROOF SUPPORT
TEMPLATES

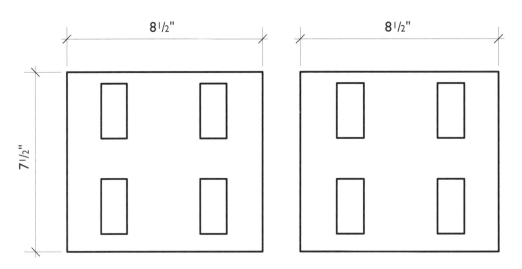

8 1/2" 8 1/2"

7 1/2"

SIDE FACADE TEMPLATES

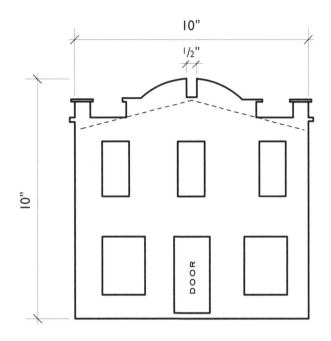

FRONT FACADE TEMPLATE

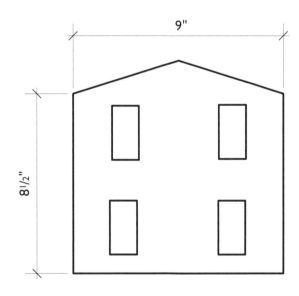

REAR FACADE TEMPLATE

FINISHED VIEW

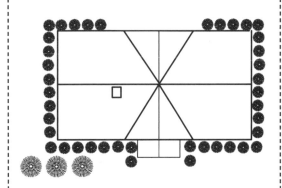

SITE WORKS

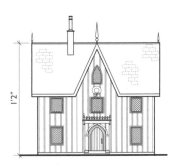

ELEVATION—
FRONT FACADE

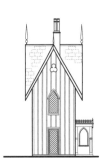

ELEVATION—
SIDE FACADE

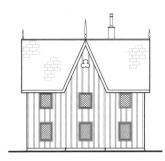

ELEVATION—
REAR FACADE

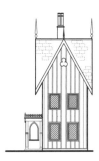

ELEVATION—
SIDE FACADE

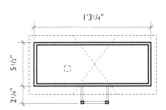

FLOOR PLAN

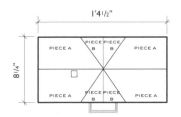

ROOF PLAN

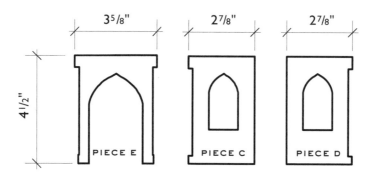

3⁵/₈" 2⁷/₈" 2⁷/₈"

4¹/₂"

PIECE E   PIECE C   PIECE D

PORCH FACADE TEMPLATES

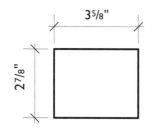

3⁵/₈"

2⁷/₈"

ENTRY PORCH ROOF TEMPLATE

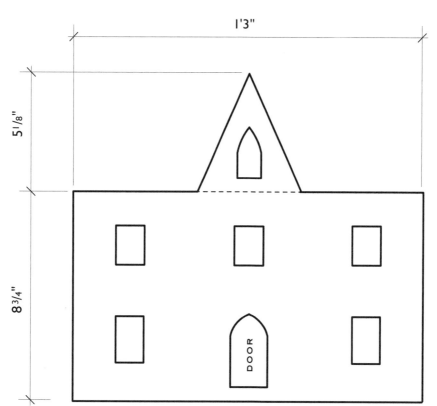

1'3"

5¹/₈"

8³/₄"

DOOR

FRONT FACADE TEMPLATE

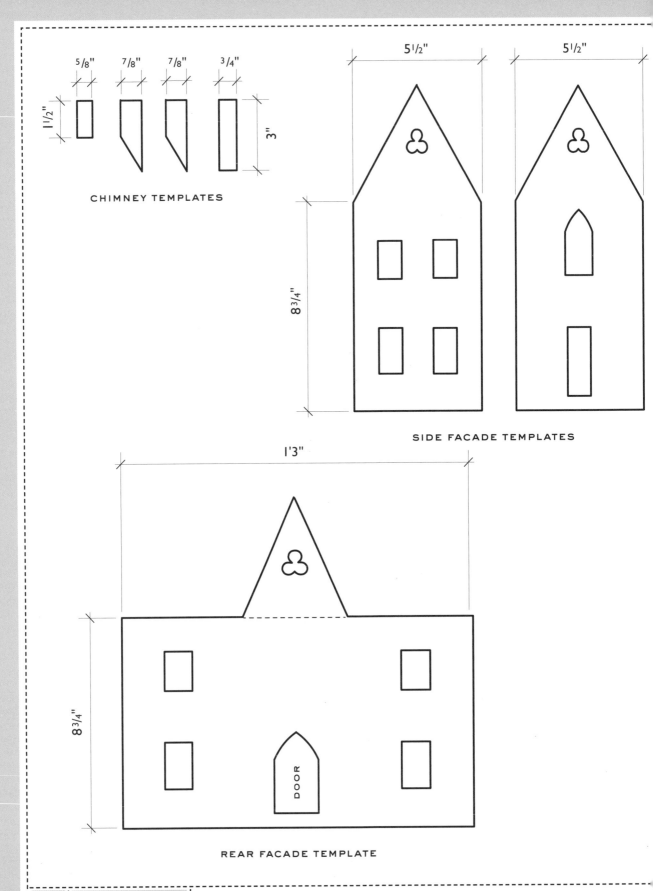

5/8"　7/8"　7/8"　3/4"

1 1/2"

3"

CHIMNEY TEMPLATES

5 1/2"　　5 1/2"

8 3/4"

SIDE FACADE TEMPLATES

1'3"

8 3/4"

DOOR

REAR FACADE TEMPLATE

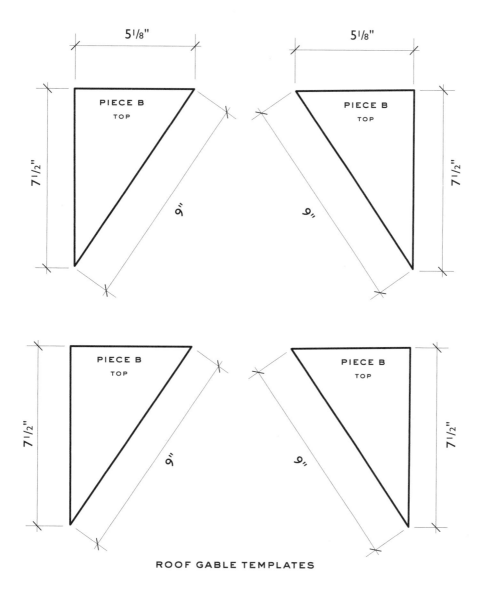

5¹/₈" 5¹/₈"

PIECE B
TOP

PIECE B
TOP

7¹/₂" 7¹/₂"

9" 9"

PIECE B
TOP

PIECE B
TOP

7¹/₂" 7¹/₂"

9" 9"

ROOF GABLE TEMPLATES

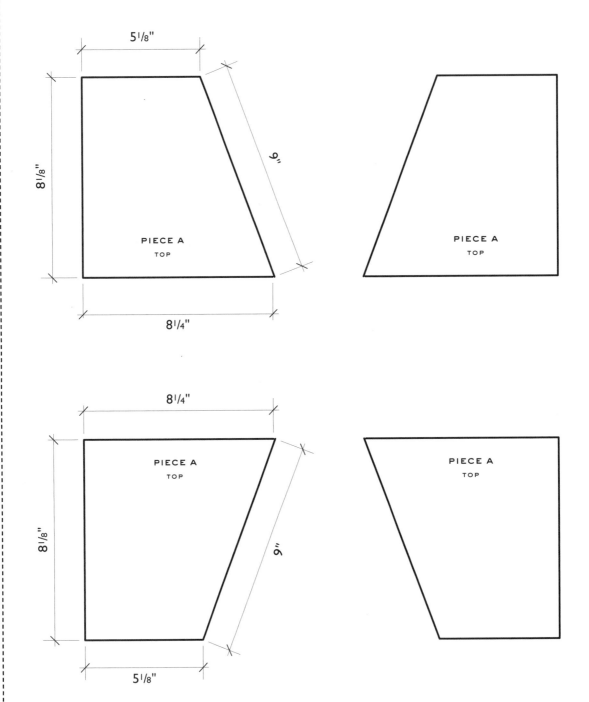

5 1/8"

8 1/8"

9"

PIECE A
TOP

8 1/4"

PIECE A
TOP

8 1/4"

PIECE A
TOP

8 1/8"

9"

5 1/8"

PIECE A
TOP

ROOF TEMPLATES

FINISHED VIEW

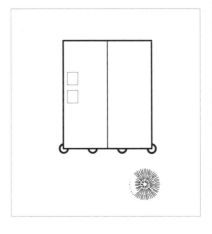

SITE WORKS

10 1/4"

ELEVATION—FRONT FACADE

ELEVATION—FRONT FACADE
WITHOUT COLUMNS

ELEVATION—SIDE FACADE

ELEVATION—REAR FACADE

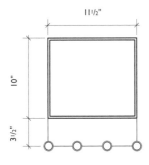

11 1/2"

10"

3 1/2"

FLOOR PLAN

ELEVATION—SIDE FACADE

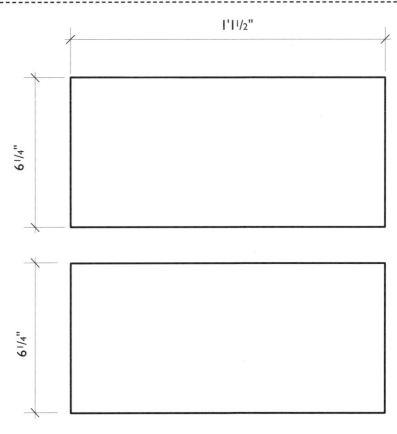

ROOF HALF TEMPLATES

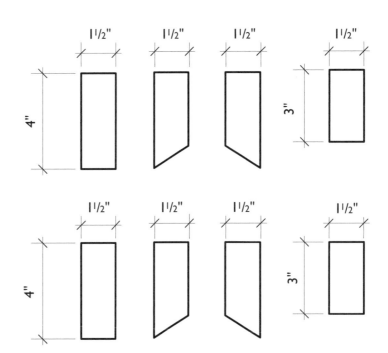

CHIMNEY TEMPLATES

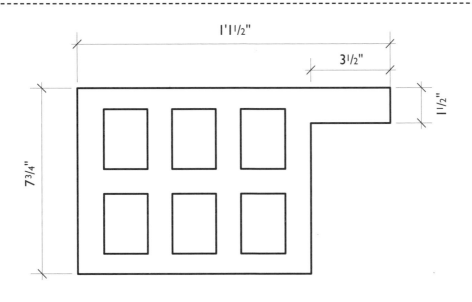

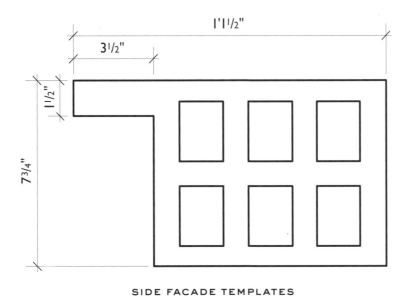

SIDE FACADE TEMPLATES

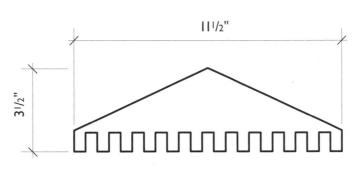

PEDIMENT TEMPLATE

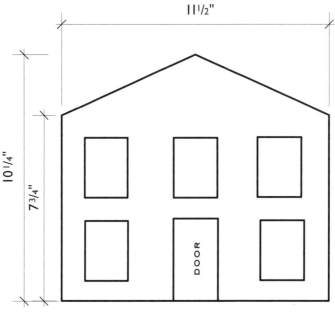

11½"

10¼"

7¾"

DOOR

REAR FACADE TEMPLATE

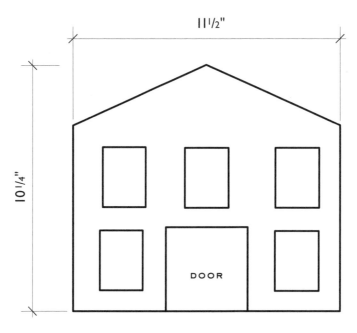

11½"

10¼"

DOOR

FRONT FACADE TEMPLATE

FINISHED VIEW

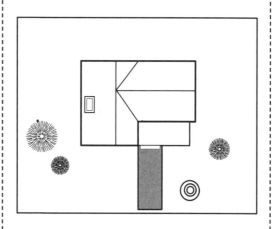

SITE WORKS

ELEVATION—FRONT FACADE

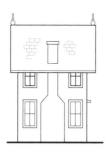

ELEVATION— SIDE FACADE

ELEVATION— REAR FACADE

ELEVATION— SIDE FACADE

BUILD INTERIOR WALL FOR ROOF SUPPORT

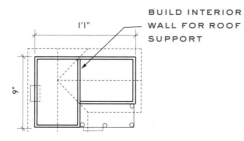

FLOOR PLAN

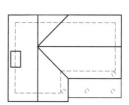

ROOF PLAN

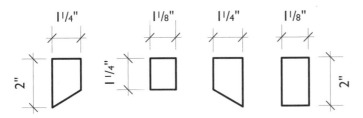

ABOVE ROOF CHIMNEY TEMPLATES

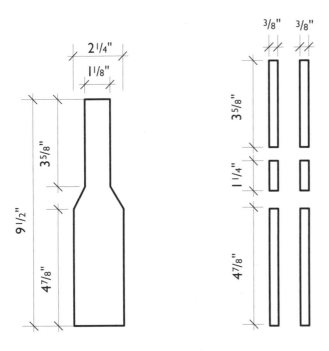

BELOW ROOF CHIMNEY TEMPLATES

NOTES: MEASURE THE HEIGHT OF THE UNDERSIDE OF THE ROOF EAVE AND TRIM THE CHIMNEY TO MEET THE UNDERSIDE OF THE EAVE. THE ANGLE OF THE CHIMNEY PIECE THAT SITS ON THE ROOF WILL NEED TO BE TRIMMED TO SIT SOLIDLY ON THE ROOF AS BUILT ROOF ANGLES WILL VARY.

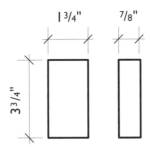

FRONT DOOR STEP TEMPLATES

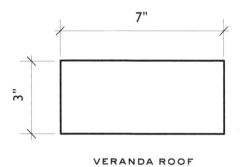

7"

3"

VERANDA ROOF

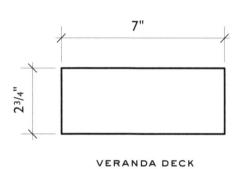

7"

2³/₄"

VERANDA DECK

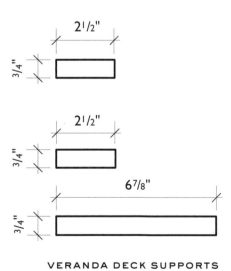

2¹/₂"

3/4"

2¹/₂"

3/4"

6⁷/₈"

3/4"

VERANDA DECK SUPPORTS

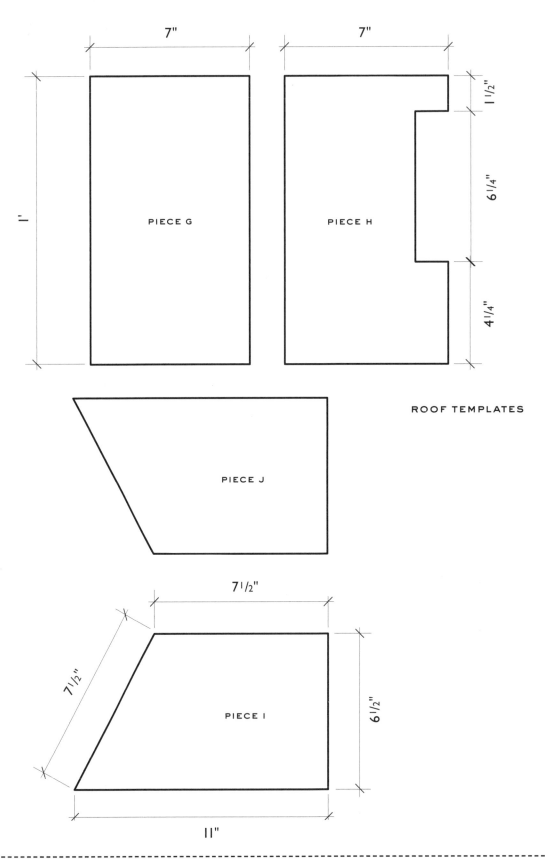

7"

7"

1 1/2"

PIECE G

PIECE H

6 1/4"

1'

4 1/4"

ROOF TEMPLATES

PIECE J

7 1/2"

7 1/2"

PIECE I

6 1/2"

11"

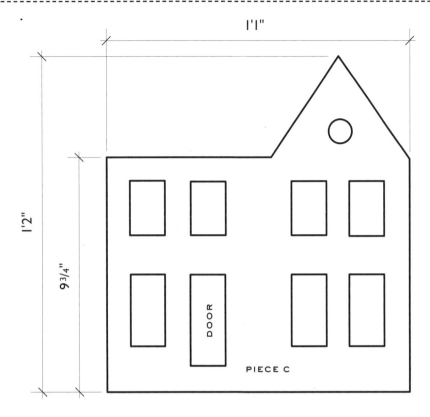

1'1"

1'2"

9³/₄"

DOOR

PIECE C

REAR FACADE TEMPLATE

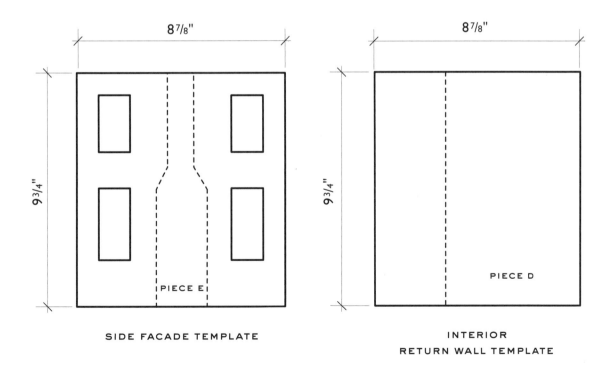

8⁷/₈"

9³/₄"

PIECE E

SIDE FACADE TEMPLATE

8⁷/₈"

9³/₄"

PIECE D

INTERIOR
RETURN WALL TEMPLATE

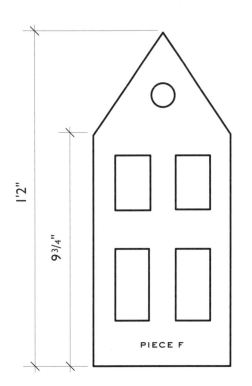

1'2"

9 3/4"

PIECE F

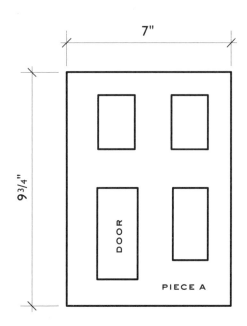

7"

9 3/4"

DOOR

PIECE A

FRONT FACADE TEMPLATES

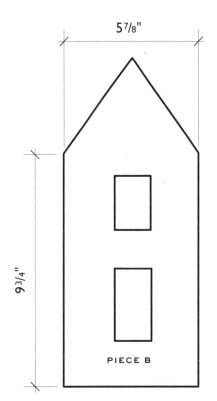

5 7/8"

9 3/4"

PIECE B

SIDE TEMPLATE

FINISHED VIEW

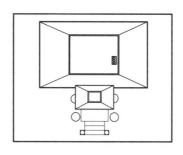

SITE WORKS

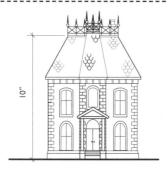

10"

ELEVATION—FRONT FACADE

ELEVATION—SIDE FACADE

ELEVATION—REAR FACADE

ELEVATION—SIDE FACADE

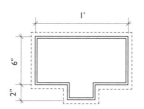

1'

6"

2"

FLOOR PLAN

ROOF PLAN

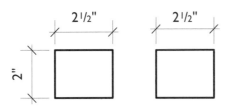

PORTICO SLOPED ROOF TEMPLATES

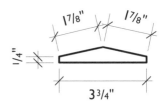

PORTICO ARCHITRAVE
TEMPLATE

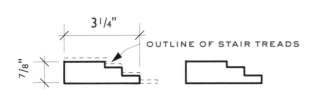

OUTLINE OF STAIR TREADS

ENTRY STAIR TEMPLATES

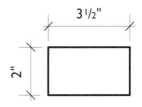

PORTICO FLAT SUPPORT
ROOF TEMPLATE

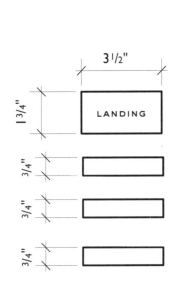

LANDING

ENTRY STAIR AND LANDING
TREAD TEMPLATE

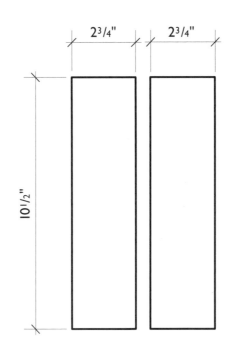

FRONT ENTRY SIDE
TEMPLATES

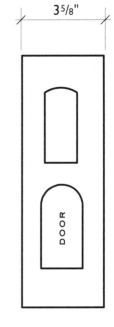

DOOR

FRONT ENTRY
TEMPLATE

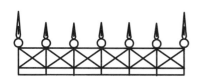

FRONT AND REAR FOR
MAIN ROOF—MAKE 2

SIDES FOR MAIN
ROOF—MAKE 2

FRONT AND REAR FOR
ENTRY ROOF—MAKE 2

SIDES FOR ENTRY
ROOF—MAKE 2

NOTE: MAKE FRETWORK WITH
ICING. DOUBLE-CHECK THE
MEASUREMENTS OF YOUR
FINISHED ROOF AND
ADJUST THE ROOF TOP
FRETWORK ACCORDINGLY.

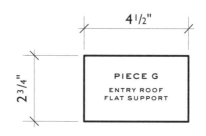

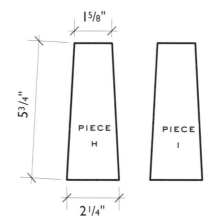

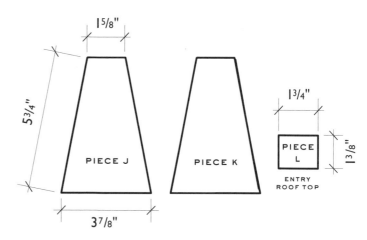

ENTRY ROOF TEMPLATES

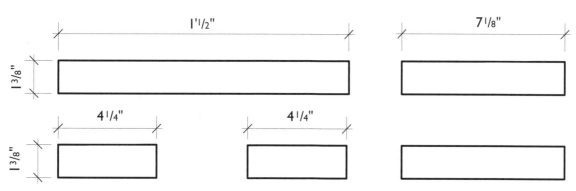

HIGH FOUNDATION BASE TEMPLATES

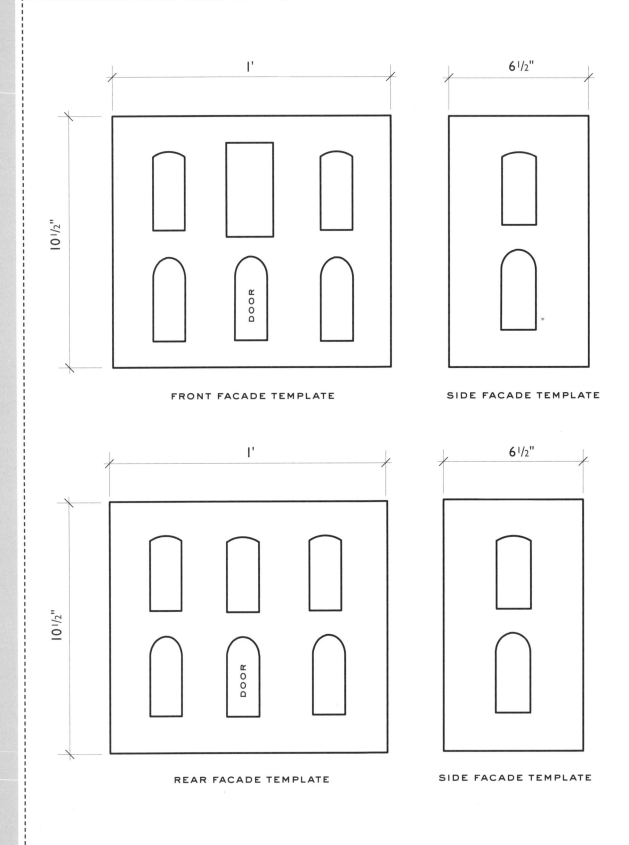

1'

6 1/2"

10 1/2"

DOOR

FRONT FACADE TEMPLATE

SIDE FACADE TEMPLATE

1'

6 1/2"

10 1/2"

DOOR

REAR FACADE TEMPLATE

SIDE FACADE TEMPLATE

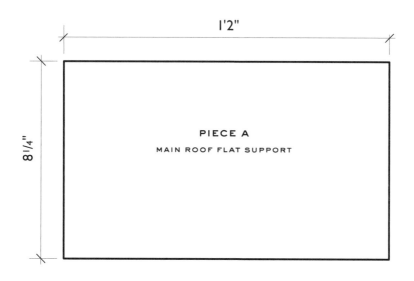

1'2"

8¹/₄"

PIECE A
MAIN ROOF FLAT SUPPORT

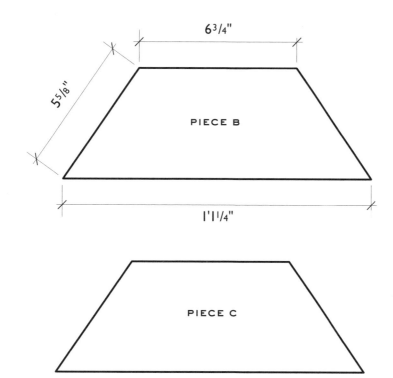

6³/₄"

5⁵/₈"

PIECE B

1'1¹/₄"

PIECE C

MAIN ROOF TEMPLATES

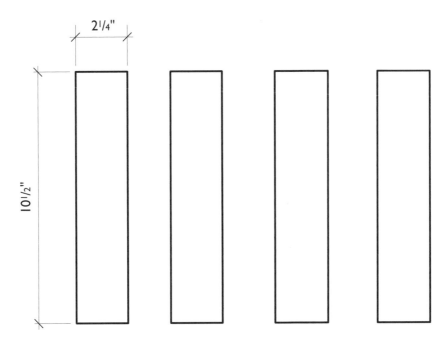

2¼"

10½"

INTERIOR ROOF SUPPORT TEMPLATES

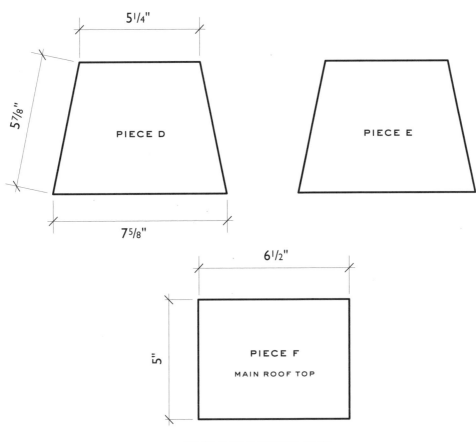

5¼"

5⅞"

PIECE D

PIECE E

7⅝"

6½"

5"

PIECE F

MAIN ROOF TOP

MAIN ROOF TEMPLATES

FINISHED VIEW

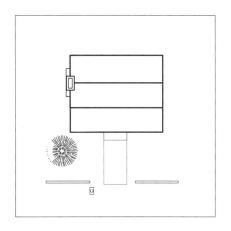

SITE WORKS

ELEVATION—FRONT FACADE

ELEVATION—SIDE FACADE

ELEVATION—REAR FACADE

ELEVATION—SIDE FACADE

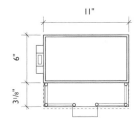

FLOOR PLAN

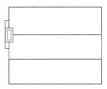

ROOF PLAN

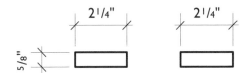

2¹/₄" 2¹/₄"

5/8"

PORCH SIDE SUPPORTS

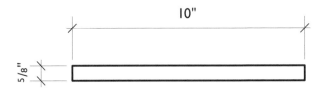

10"

5/8"

PORCH REAR SUPPORT TEMPLATE

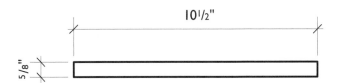

10¹/₂"

5/8"

PORCH FRONT SUPPORT TEMPLATE

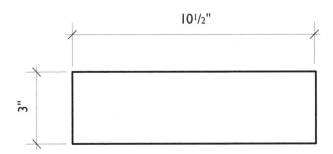

10¹/₂"

3"

PORCH DECK TEMPLATE

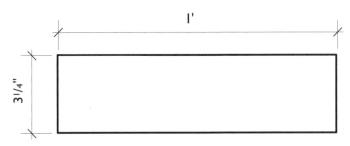

1'

3¹/₄"

PORCH ROOF TEMPLATE

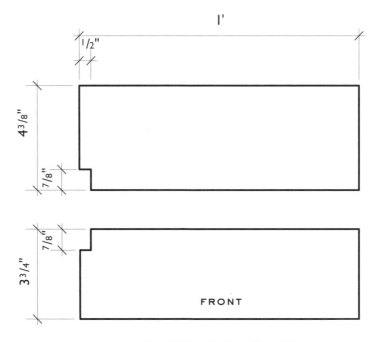

ROOF HALF TEMPLATES

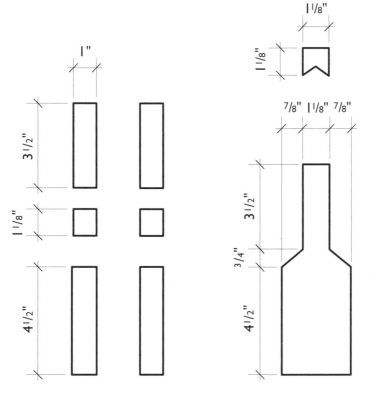

CHIMNEY TEMPLATES

NOTE: BE PREPARED TO TRIM THE ROOF CUT OUT FROM THE CHIMNEY TO FIT YOUR CHIMNEY WITH THE CANDY FINISH.

MAKE THE CHIMNEY TEMPLATE NARROWER IF YOU WISH TO USE CHOCOLATE ROCK CANDY

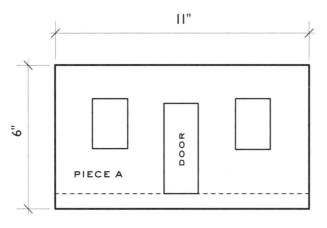

FRONT FACADE TEMPLATE

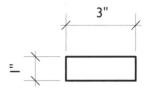

FRONT STEP TEMPLATE

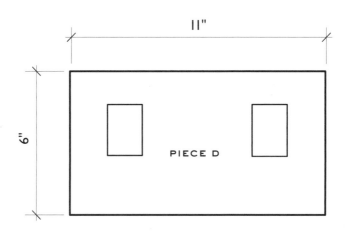

REAR FACADE TEMPLATE

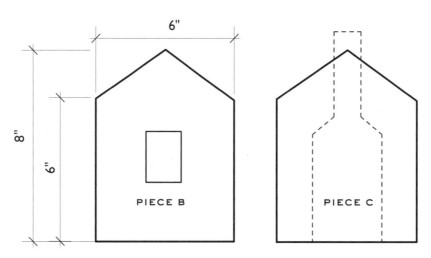

SIDE FACADE TEMPLATES

FINISHED VIEW

SITE WORKS

ELEVATION—FRONT FACADE

1'3 1/2"

ELEVATION—SIDE FACADE

ELEVATION—REAR FACADE

ELEVATION—SIDE FACADE

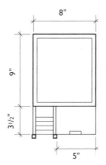

FLOOR PLAN

8"

9"

3 1/2"

5"

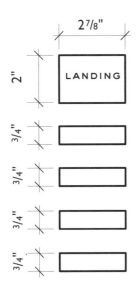

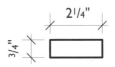

STEP DOWN
TO RECESSED AREA

STAIR LANDING AND
TREAD TEMPLATES

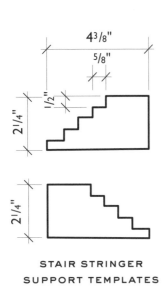

STAIR STRINGER
SUPPORT TEMPLATES

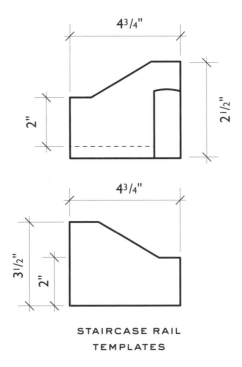

STAIRCASE RAIL
TEMPLATES

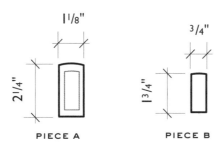

1 1/8"

2 1/4"

PIECE A

3/4"

1 3/4"

PIECE B

CELLAR DOOR TEMPLATES

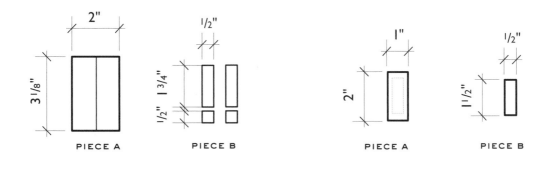

2"

3 1/8"

PIECE A

1/2"

1/2" 1 3/4"

PIECE B

FRONT DOOR TEMPLATES

1"

2"

PIECE A

1/2"

1 1/2"

PIECE B

REAR DOOR TEMPLATES

NOTE: MAKE DOORS AND CORNICE WITH PASTILLAGE.

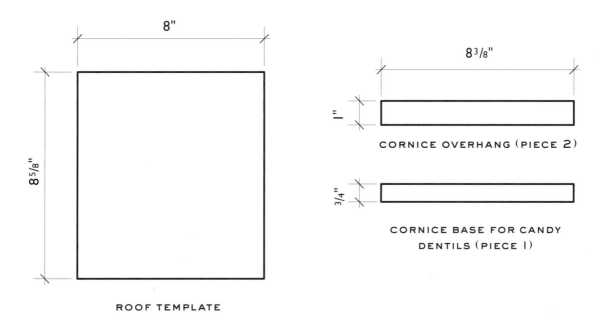

8"

8 5/8"

ROOF TEMPLATE

8 3/8"

1"

CORNICE OVERHANG (PIECE 2)

3/4"

CORNICE BASE FOR CANDY
DENTILS (PIECE 1)

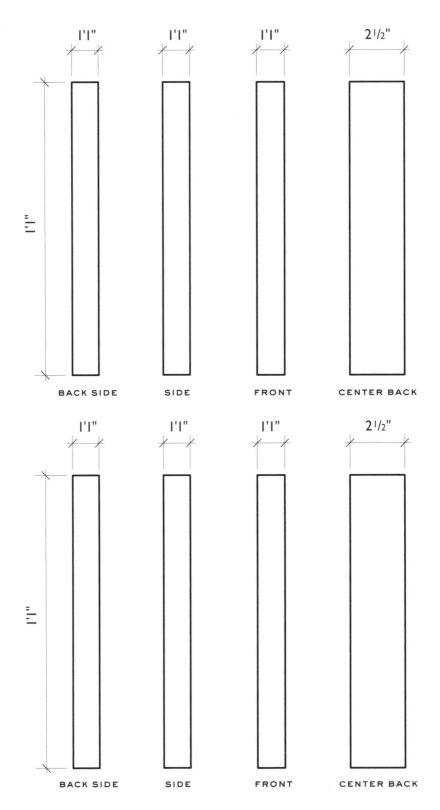

1'1"   1'1"   1'1"   2½"

1'1"

BACK SIDE   SIDE   FRONT   CENTER BACK

1'1"   1'1"   1'1"   2½"

1'1"

BACK SIDE   SIDE   FRONT   CENTER BACK

ROOF SUPPORTS

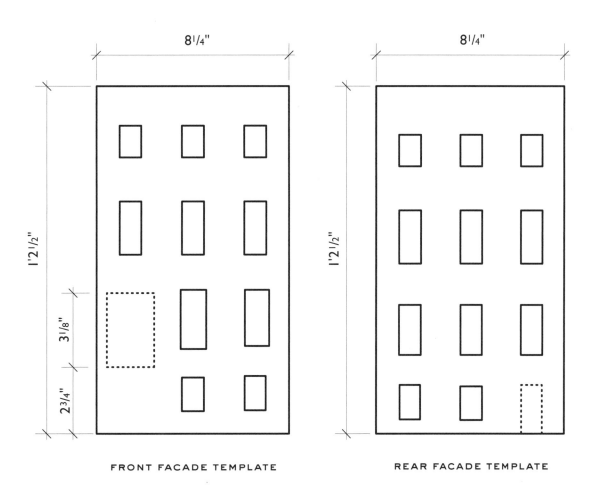

8¹/₄"

8¹/₄"

1'2¹/₂"

1'2¹/₂"

3¹/₈"

2³/₄"

FRONT FACADE TEMPLATE

REAR FACADE TEMPLATE

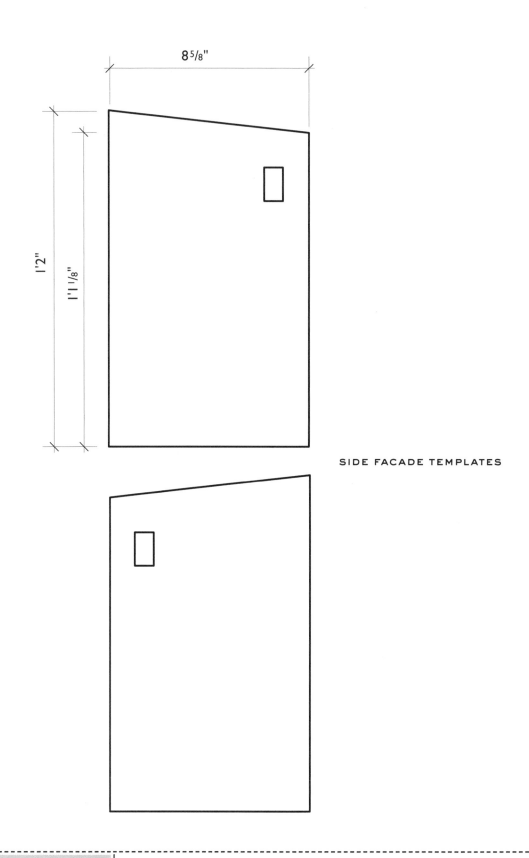

8 5/8"

1'2"

1'1 1/8"

SIDE FACADE TEMPLATES

FINISHED VIEW

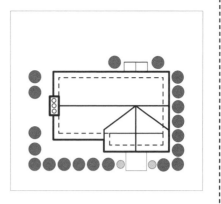

SITE WORKS

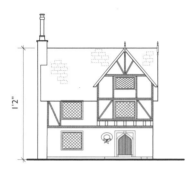

ELEVATION—FRONT FACADE

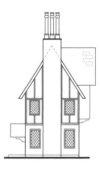

ELEVATION—SIDE FACADE

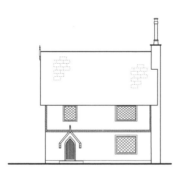

ELEVATION—REAR FACADE

ELEVATION—SIDE FACADE

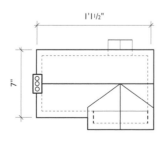

FLOOR PLAN

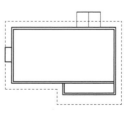

ROOF PLAN

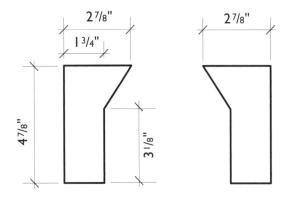

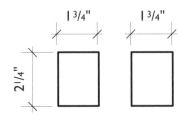

BACK DOOR ROOF TEMPLATES

OVERHANG SIDE TEMPLATES

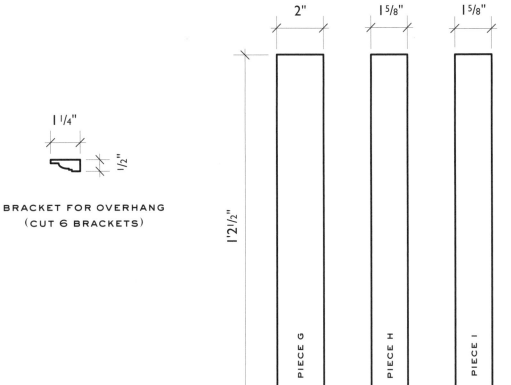

1¼"

½"

BRACKET FOR OVERHANG
(CUT 6 BRACKETS)

2"

1⅝"

1⅝"

1'2½"

PIECE G

PIECE H

PIECE I

FULL-HEIGHT CHIMNEY TEMPLATES

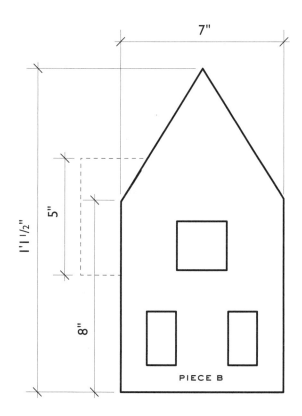

7"

1'1 1/2"

5"

8"

PIECE B

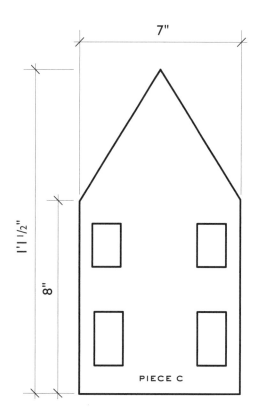

7"

1'1 1/2"

8"

PIECE C

SIDE FACADE TEMPLATES

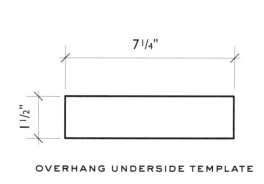

7 1/4"

1 1/2"

OVERHANG UNDERSIDE TEMPLATE

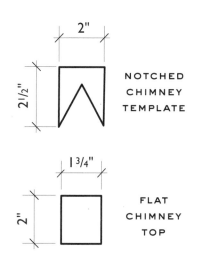

2"

2 1/2"

NOTCHED
CHIMNEY
TEMPLATE

1 3/4"

2"

FLAT
CHIMNEY
TOP

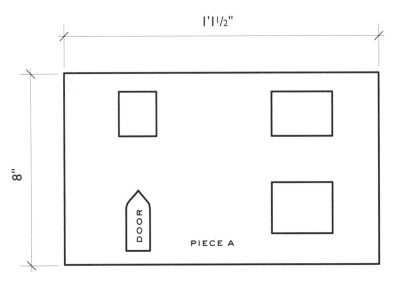

1'1½"

8"

DOOR

PIECE A

REAR FACADE

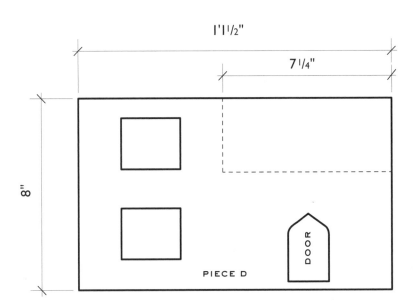

1'1½"

7¼"

8"

DOOR

PIECE D

FRONT FACADE

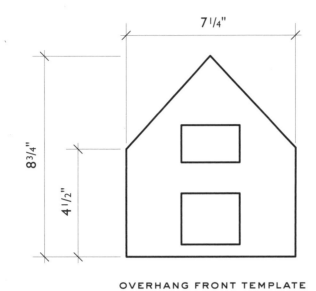

OVERHANG FRONT TEMPLATE

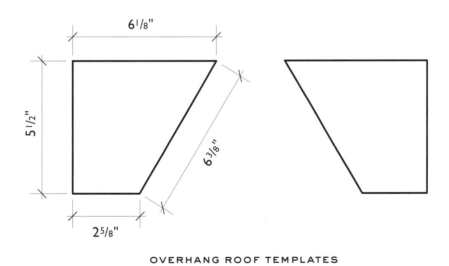

OVERHANG ROOF TEMPLATES

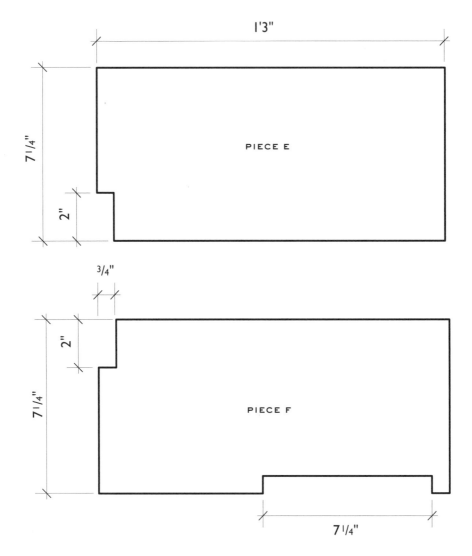

1'3"

7 1/4"

2"

PIECE E

3/4"

2"

7 1/4"

PIECE F

7 1/4"

ROOF TEMPLATES

FINISHED VIEW

SITE WORKS

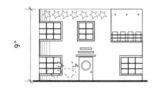

ELEVATION—FRONT FACADE

ELEVATION—SIDE FACADE

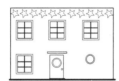

ELEVATION—REAR FACADE

ELEVATION—SIDE FACADE

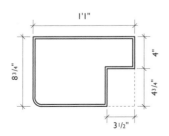

FLOOR PLAN

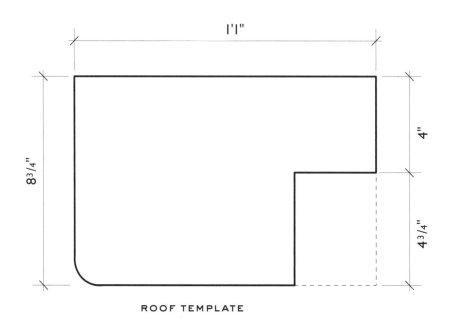

1'1"

8³/₄"

4"

4³/₄"

ROOF TEMPLATE

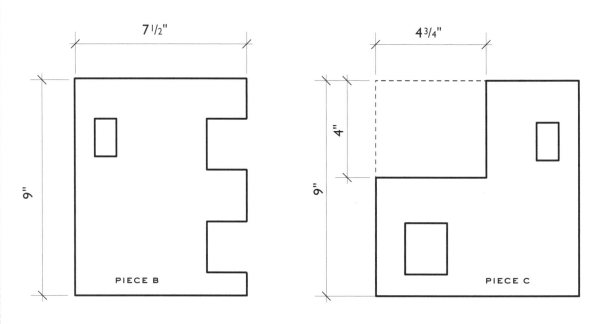

7¹/₂"

9"

PIECE B

4³/₄"

4"

9"

PIECE C

SIDE FACADE TEMPLATES

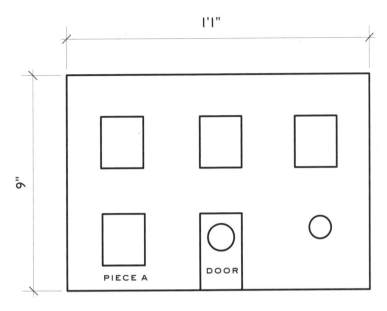

1'1"

9"

PIECE A

DOOR

REAR FACADE TEMPLATE

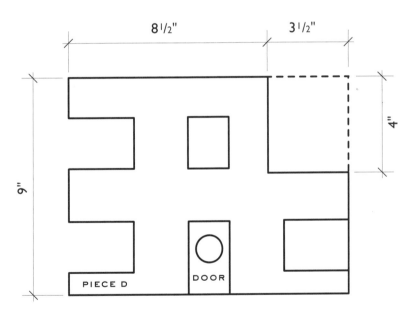

8 1/2"

3 1/2"

9"

4"

PIECE D

DOOR

FRONT FACADE TEMPLATE

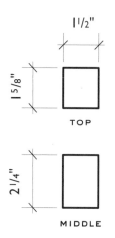

1½"

1 5/8"

TOP

2¼"

MIDDLE

7/8"

BOTTOM

CURVE TEMPLATES

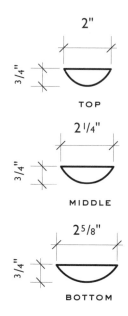

2"

3/4"

TOP

2¼"

3/4"

MIDDLE

2 5/8"

3/4"

BOTTOM

ABOVE-DOOR TRIM TEMPLATES

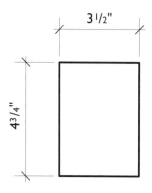

3½"

4 3/4"

TERRACE FLOOR TEMPLATE

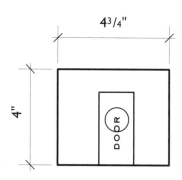

4 3/4"

4"

DOOR

TERRACE BACK WALL TEMPLATE

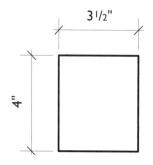

3½"

4"

TERRACE SIDE WALL TEMPLATE

2"

FLAMINGO TEMPLATES

FINISHED VIEW

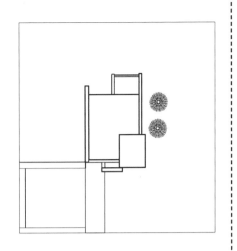

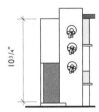

ELEVATION—FRONT FACADE

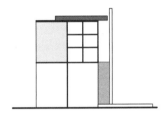

ELEVATION—SIDE FACADE

THREE
SEPARATE
HARD CANDY
GLASS
WINDOWS

ELEVATION—REAR FACADE

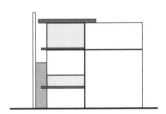

ELEVATION—SIDE FACADE

FLOOR PLAN

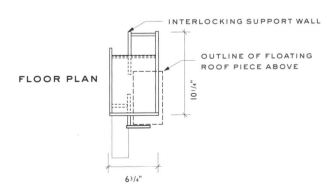

INTERLOCKING SUPPORT WALL

OUTLINE OF FLOATING
ROOF PIECE ABOVE

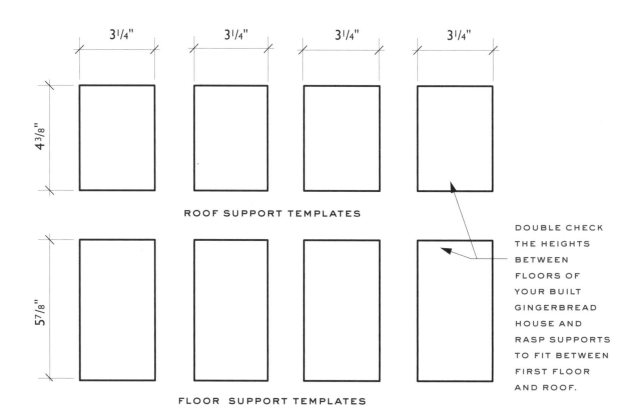

3¼"   3¼"   3¼"   3¼"

4³⁄₈"

ROOF SUPPORT TEMPLATES

DOUBLE CHECK THE HEIGHTS BETWEEN FLOORS OF YOUR BUILT GINGERBREAD HOUSE AND RASP SUPPORTS TO FIT BETWEEN FIRST FLOOR AND ROOF.

5⁷⁄₈"

FLOOR SUPPORT TEMPLATES

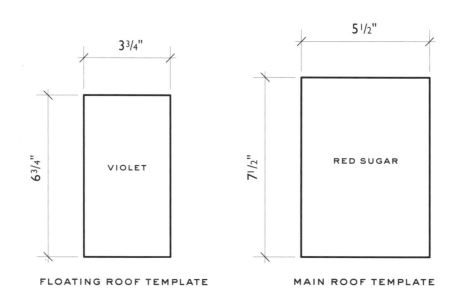

3³⁄₄"

6³⁄₄"

VIOLET

FLOATING ROOF TEMPLATE

5½"

7½"

RED SUGAR

MAIN ROOF TEMPLATE

3"

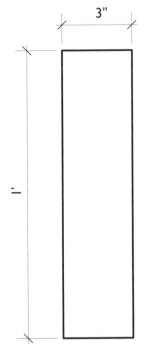

1'

FLOATING FRONT WALL
TEMPLATE

2"

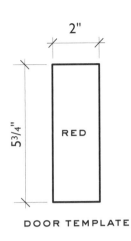

5³/₄"

RED

DOOR TEMPLATE

3"

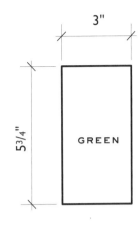

5³/₄"

GREEN

ENTRY RETURN WALL TEMPLATE
ADJACENT TO DOOR

5⁷/₈"

3¹/₄"   2⁵/₈"

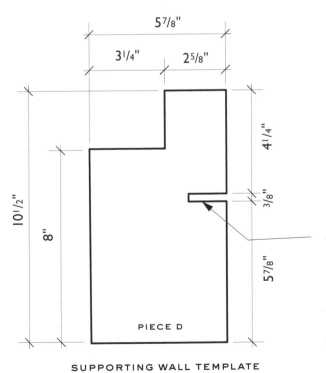

4¹/₄"

3/₈"

10¹/₂"

8"

5⁷/₈"

PIECE D

SUPPORTING WALL TEMPLATE

INTERSECTING WALL
THAT SUPPORTS THE
REAR ELEVATION

BE PREPARED TO TRIM
THE INTERSECTING
NOTCH TO FIT AROUND
THE FIRST FLOOR.

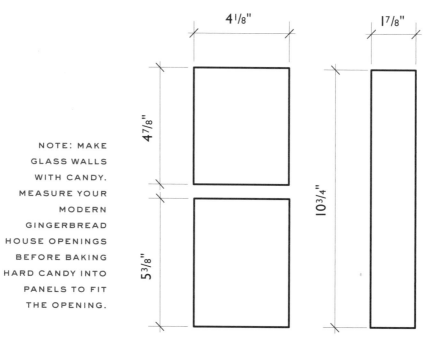

NOTE: MAKE GLASS WALLS WITH CANDY. MEASURE YOUR MODERN GINGERBREAD HOUSE OPENINGS BEFORE BAKING HARD CANDY INTO PANELS TO FIT THE OPENING.

4 1/8"

4 7/8"

5 3/8"

1 7/8"

10 3/4"

REAR FACADE GLASS PANEL TEMPLATES

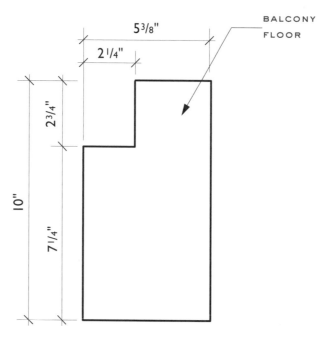

5 3/8"

2 1/4"

BALCONY FLOOR

2 3/4"

10"

7 1/4"

SECOND-STORY FLOOR TEMPLATE

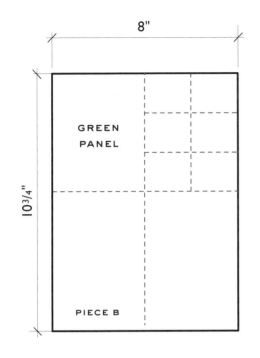

SIDE PANEL TEMPLATE

8"

10³/₄"

GREEN
PANEL

PIECE B

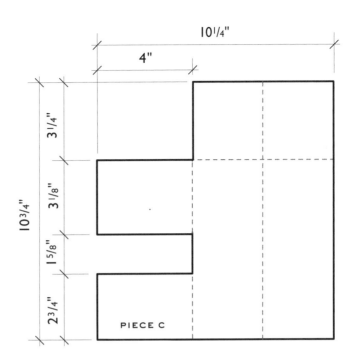

SIDE PANEL TEMPLATE

10¹/₄"

4"

10³/₄"

3¹/₄"

3¹/₈"

1⁵/₈"

2³/₄"

PIECE C

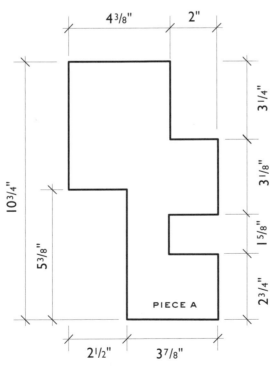

FRONT FACADE TEMPLATE

4³/₈"   2"

10³/₄"

5³/₈"

3¹/₄"

3¹/₈"

1⁵/₈"

2³/₄"

PIECE A

2¹/₂"   3⁷/₈"

GLOSSARY OF ARCHITECTURAL TERMS

ARCHITRAVE The lowest part of a classical entablature, resting on columns.

BATTEN BOARDS Wooden strips arranged vertically as siding.

CHIMNEY POT A cylindrical earthenware or metal pipe fitted on the top of a chimney to disperse smoke.

CORBELS Short horizontal timbers supporting a girder.

CORNICE A prominent, continuous, horizontally projecting feature surmounting a wall or other construction or dividing it horizontally for compositional purposes.

CRENELLATED Notched, as is the top edge of the wall of a castle.

CUPOLA A small dome set atop a roof.

DENTIL A series of closely spaced small blocks, often used in classical architecture beneath a cornice.

DORMERS Small gables projecting from a sloping roof.

ENTABLATURE The upper section of a classical building, resting on the columns and constituting the architrave, frieze, and cornice.

FALSE HALF-TIMBERING Heavy beams filled in with masonry serving a decorative rather than a structural purpose.

FRIEZE Any decorative band above a cornice.

GABLE The portion of the front or side of a building enclosed by or masking the end of a pitched roof.

MULLIONED WINDOWS Windows vertically and horizontally divided by thin strips of wood.

PARAPET A low protective wall at the edge of a balcony or roof.

PEDIMENT The triangular part of a Greek temple (or a house built to look like one) between the columns and the eaves, usually decorated with sculpture in low relief.

PEDIMENTED GABLE A low triangular gable surmounting a colonnade, or an imitation of this, used to crown a doorway.

PILASTERS Shallow columns projecting from a wall, with a capital and a base.

PINNACLES Small upright structures rising above the roof of a building or capping a tower or other projecting architectural element.

PORTICO A roof supported by columns or piers, usually attached to a building as a porch.

RUSTICATION A boldly textured surface of rough-hewn blocks.

STICKWORK Wooden beams filled in with masonry or plaster to decorate the facade of a house; similar to half-timbering.

VIGAS Heavy timbers used as supports in Pueblo-style homes.

ACKNOWLEDGMENTS

Thanks to Jennifer Griffin for handing over her idea for a different type of gingerbread house book. Thanks to Sharon Bowers for bringing us together to work on this wonderfully fun project. And thanks to both for shepherding it to Rica Allannic at Clarkson Potter. Rica's enthusiasm and commitment have been an inspiration. At Potter, Kathleen Fleury took care of so many important details along the way. A million thanks to Ashley Phillips and Sibylle Kazeroid, who checked and double-checked about that many details in the manuscript and drawings so the recipes and templates will work for our readers at home. Laura Palese and Jane Treuhaft made sure this book was as beautiful in reality as it was in our mind's eye.

Katherine Yang did a fantastic job of re-creating the houses for the photographs, and helped us perfect the recipes as she worked. Alexandra Grablewski's glowing photographs perfectly captured the distinct personalities and telling details of each house. Thanks to Todd Bonné for his assistance at the shoots and to Fuel Digital for final imaging help.

Finally, thanks to our families, Paul and Claire Judice and Jack, Rose, and Eve Bishop, for all of their ideas, practical help, and patience as these gingerbread houses took over our kitchens and our lives.

INDEX

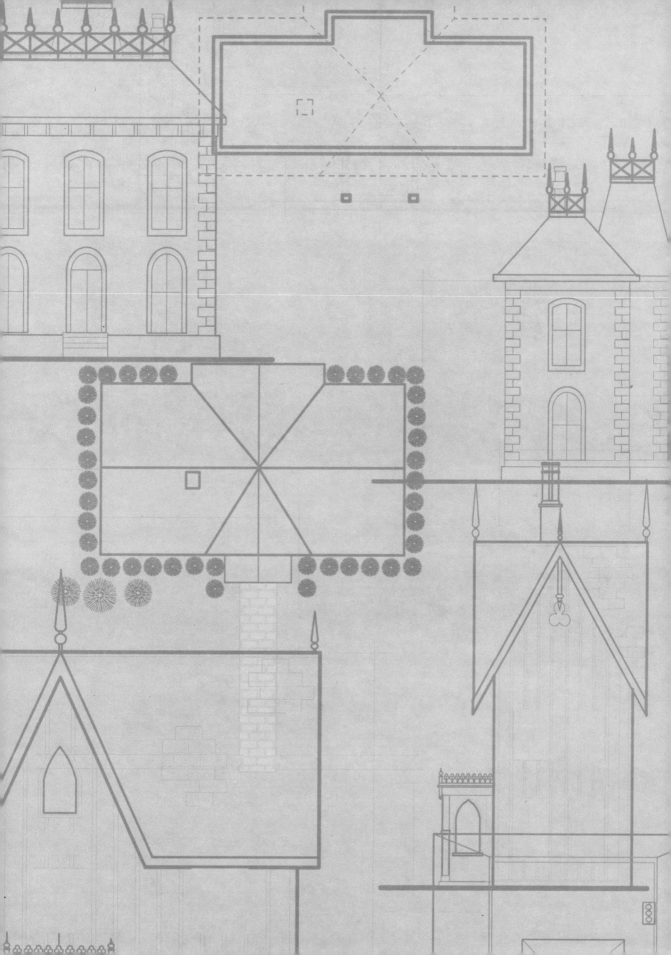

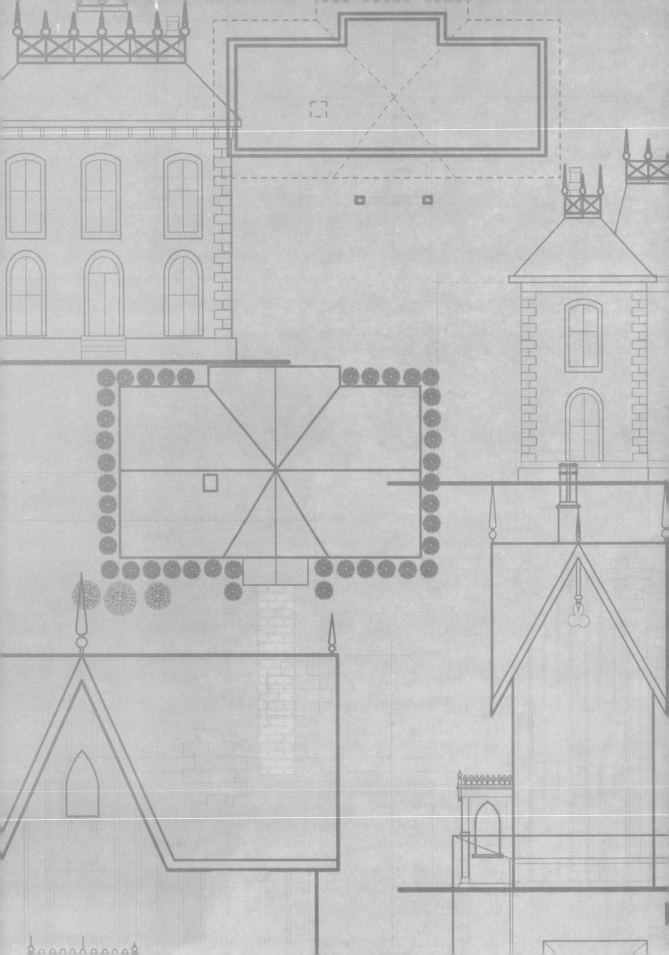